When They Took Dad Away

Barbara McGillicuddy Bolton

North Country Press

When They Took Dad Away

Copyright © 2019 by Barbara McGillicuddy Bolton

ISBN 978-1-943424-50-4

Library of Congress Control Number: 2019947786

North Country Press
Unity, Maine

For Frank

Prologue

In Bath, Maine, where we did our shopping and attended church, my family were outsiders. Across the river in Woolwich, where our little house hugged a rise on the corner of the Barley Neck Road and Route One, we were also outsiders, having lived there a scant two years.

We had all been born two hundred miles north in or just outside Houlton, the county seat of Aroostook, my father and mother in October of 1908, five days apart, so close that when they went to St. Mary's Church in Houlton to prepare for their wedding in 1935, their baptism certificates turned up next to each other. Tommy, for six years their only child, was born in 1936, during the Depression, when (my mother told me after I'd grown up) she and my father had to be very, very careful not to conceive again. (I lacked the temerity to ask her to spell out how she and my father went about being "careful.") Clement was born in 1942 and I in 1943 when he was still only crawling — at fourteen months he was a late walker. My mother told me — again when I was grown up — that she'd been miffed when another woman commented that couples were having babies one right after the other to avoid the draft. (If that was true in my parents' case, it worked. While my father's two unmarried brothers were called up, Dad was not, and Mum said he'd been terrified he might be.) In 1946, Charlie, our future baby boomer and Vietnam vet, completed the family.

It was the future that brought us to Woolwich in 1950. We had been living for three years farther northwest in Patten, where Dad was the town manager. With a population of approximately 1,000 to Woolwich's approximately 2,000 but with no Bath nearby offering churches, stores, and a library among other amenities, Patten relied upon its own main street with its own small establishments. It was the entrance to the Allagash, a wilderness waterway, and where both locals and "sports" could equip themselves for a trek. The economy was based on lumber and guiding. There was an element of the Wild West in the place that even a child could spot. My little friends spoke of game wardens who went about applying the law to how many deer a man could shoot and under what circumstance, as though they were public enemies. (I was an adult before it occurred to me that a game warden could be an upstanding person.) One day I witnessed the father of a classmate of mine get into a fistfight with another man in the middle of Main Street. People said the fight was over the wife of one of the men.

Marriages took place young in Patten, and many were of the shotgun variety. These were arguing points with which my father hooked my mother: we kids wouldn't become tempted into premature sexual activity or immature marriages. We'd have advantages; we'd go to college as my mother had done. And there'd be the money to do it because my father wouldn't be relying on a salary but would be running his own lucrative business. He'd own and operate a greenhouse.

Down the slope from our little house in Woolwich, on level ground next to Route One, squatted the greenhouse, one of the few commercial establishments in a town with one hundred miles of road but no center. Atop a boulder, its crevices bursting with colorful annuals, stood a white sign with a green shamrock and green lettering proclaiming *McGillicuddy Florist* and below that in smaller print: *cead mile failte,* which meant, we kids were told, "A hundred thousand welcomes." My father didn't speak Gaelic, nor did his parents, nor his parents' parents nor anyone else as far back as we knew. Occasionally, misled by the sign, someone came into the greenhouse exclaiming in Gaelic, and my father would have a fine time laughing and chatting with the visitor — in English. Then it was back to the unrelenting work of the greenhouse.

The greenhouse ran us. During the Woolwich years, Charlie's birthday was too close to Memorial Day to be celebrated with cake and candles and presents. Thanksgiving, Christmas, Easter, Mothers' Day, Memorial Day, the Fourth of July and all the days leading up to the holidays, my father and Tommy spent arranging and delivering flowers, with Mum providing meals at all hours. Spring was busy with planting the field-sized gardens, summer with tending them, fall with harvesting and winter with trying to make grow under glass what had previously grown out of doors.

There were two structures of glass — the greenhouse itself and a smaller one called an orlight. (Dad loved using correct terms; the orlight was always an orlight, never a small greenhouse.) The orlight and the greenhouse proper were entered through the office, a one-room wooden building with long counters for arranging bouquets and sprays and tall glass-doored refrigerators for cut flowers, of which I thought the fresh-faced, spicy carnations the very best and in comparison to which the neatly folded up roses looked prim, the extravagant gladiolas garish, the earthy geraniums like roosters' combs. Ivy climbed from a pot on one of the counters to where the wall met the ceiling and wound itself nearly all around the entire office.

In front of the office, down a few steps, a circular drive arced around the green and white sign — *cead mile failte!* — making it very easy, natural even, for the drivers of cars to slow down, enter on one side of the sign, sweep around to the entrance, climb a couple of steps, stroll into the office, buy a bunch of flowers on impulse (whatever was fresh, plentiful and expensive), make an exit out the other side of the drive and shoot off up the highway.

This didn't happen often. Aside from the frantic holiday rushes and in spite of all the hard work, business was slow. On the other hand, maybe it wasn't the business that was failing; maybe it was Daddy himself, Daddy's mind. Maybe everything would have worked out okay if Daddy had been okay, if some glitch in his thinking or his hormones or his DNA, derived partly from a strand of familial melancholia, over-excitability or plain craziness, hadn't overtaken him and culminated in one momentous day.

The day they took Daddy away.

1

The Day

On the morning of that Sunday, the whole family climbs into our green Kaiser-Frazer and rides the four miles to St. Mary's in Bath for Mass. At the wheel is either Daddy, in his suit and fedora, or Tommy, at fifteen the size of an adult — a tall adult — and a driver ever since he got his permit almost two years ago. Mumma, wearing a good dress, sits between them on the bench seat — in 1952, all front seats are bench seats. Perched on her perm is one of those bird's-nest hats of the time, its black netting pushed up off her eyes. Clement, Charlie and I are in the back. I'm wearing a child's version of the bird's nest hat and a good dress, no doubt one Mumma has "run up" on her sewing machine. If Mumma has curled my hair, the moist salt air will straighten it by midday. Clement has one of the windows — there would be no peace if he were made to share this privilege the way Charlie and I do. Privately, I think it would look a little nicer if I as the only girl sat between my parents in the front seat, but I'm only too aware of the unspoken assumption that if Tommy and Clement were to share the back seat they might get into a scuffle. My brothers wear neatly ironed shirts and pressed cotton pants. I often hear people comment on how good-looking each of them is and do not yet realize that I am rather plain in comparison.

When we come to the cemetery we kids all take deep breaths and say, "Beebeebeebee," not inhaling the whole time until we come to the end of the fence surrounding the tombstones and shout, "Peter Rabbit!" Tommy has taught us younger kids this practice along with other bits of knowledge such as that if we snuffle snot instead of blowing it out into a hankie it will ascend to our brains and swim around there until we die.

The conversation in the car is loud. Our family always talks loudly wherever we are because we want to include Mumma, who's hard of hearing. Although Daddy has never completely adjusted to Mumma's handicap, we kids grew up learning to look right at her when we speak, to make our voices fuller rather than shriller, and to use a different word if she gets stuck on one. We're used to touching her hand and repeating what people outside the family say to her; sometimes it's enough just to supply her with a key word. And we kids all talk loudly the way she does. At Central School, my classmates smile when it's my turn to read because I do so at the top of my voice. Although Mumma has trouble hearing voices on the phone, the person on the other end has no such problem because Mumma always shouts into the instrument.

That's another thing we kids learned growing up: people who are hard of hearing don't hear their own voices well. Some talk too low to be understood; others shout. Mumma is a shouter, especially when she becomes animated. We kids learned to touch her arm with one hand and hold the other hand at chest level and slowly drop it. Then Mumma says, "Oh, oh," and lowers her volume. Sometimes we do it at Mass when her singing rises above the rest of the congregation.

If Tommy is serving Mass, we've come early enough for him to go into the sacristy and slip on his black and white vestments. In the missal I got for First Communion, its hard white cover as shiny as a mirror, the Ordinary of the Mass appears in two languages side by side, and so when the priest and Tommy begin in Latin, I can follow in English. *I will go to the altar of God/ To God, who gives joy to my youth.* Kneeling erectly, sitting or walking, his black hair slicked to one side, joyfully attentive to the duties of an altar boy — ringing a bell, swinging a censor — Tommy looks like Boy, the teenaged hero of a comic book series. Despite his youth, Boy comes to the rescue of anyone in peril and restores justice. From the time we were little, if Clement hurt me and I ran to Mumma, she would remonstrate with him and say, "Oh, don't hurt little sister. Love little sister." If I appealed to Tommy, however, Clement got paid back. One afternoon the summer before, Tommy took Clement and Charlie and me across the Barley Neck Road to a little bridge over Route One for the first swim of the season. Over the course of the winter, my prowess having built up in my own mind, I had bragged I could swim. As Charlie and I sat on the sandy bank dipping our toes while our older brothers swam about, I was having my doubts. Suddenly Clement grabbed my hand and pulled me in over my head. "Let's see you swim," he yelled. No swimmer after all, I flailed and swallowed water and choked, holding onto Clement's head, and we both might have drowned if Tommy hadn't powered over from the middle of the stream and pulled me to safety. Once I was on shore, shuddering and weeping, he went after Clement, grabbed him in a choke hold and held him underwater for a suitable length of time to restore justice. To me, except for the trained monkey that wreathed the comic book hero's shoulders, Tommy is Boy — and he'd be good with a monkey if he had one.

Until this year of that Sunday, I stayed in the pew while Clement and sometimes my parents joined the Communion line. I used to watch the procession of big girls down from the choir loft, their hands folded, heads bowed, and, although I know a great deal about boys of various ages, I wondered what it would be like to be, say, an eleven-year-old girl. This year I receive Communion with the big kids.

After Mass we drive back to Woolwich for our Sunday dinner at the dining table, which — there being no dining room — is in one corner of the living room, a huge room in a small house. Mumma usually makes a roast that she can use as the base for creative leftovers the rest of the week. We have baked potatoes with gravy and a green vegetable and, for dessert, one of Mumma's pies or cakes or a pan of squares, taken up in the kitchen with a spatula and served on a decorative plate.

Clement and I remain in our dress-up clothes because we have to be back at St. Mary's for Sunday School at two. Sometimes Tommy or Daddy drives us, although lately we've been taking the Greyhound bus that stops at one o'clock on Route One across from the greenhouse and leaves us off close enough to walk the rest of the way. As third and fourth graders, we're old enough to travel alone, and, besides, we have each other. And, besides that, the greenhouse keeps Daddy and Tommy, his right-hand man, busy seven days a week.

Each Sunday School class occupies a section of the pews. Not having a parish school — although with ample financial resources to build and maintain one — is a point of pride with Father Maney, our miserly pastor. I look longingly over where Sister Isidore, my last year's teacher, is preparing the second graders to make First Communion. Sister is young — we can see that despite the white wimple and black veil that surround her angelic face — and sweet-natured. Every Sunday we finished the class convinced of her — and by extension, God's — loving regard for us. This year's Sister is also nice but does not make Sister Isidore's lasting impression.

After instruction, all classes remain in place for the benediction and litany performed by the curate with the euphonious name of Father Bellefontaine — and referred to by Father Maney from the pulpit as "the little fellow." I am mesmerized by the smoke and incense coming from the swung censor, by the late afternoon light slanting through the stained glass windows, by our repetition of the chants *ora pro nobis* and *orate pro nobis.*

There is no Greyhound bus to oblige us on the return trip, and so no matter how we got to Sunday School, Daddy or Tommy must pick us up and take us home. This afternoon we don't spot the green Kaiser-Frazer anywhere. That's not unusual. Sometimes the greenhouse is so busy we have to wait a few minutes or even up to half an hour. But we've never been forgotten.

Until possibly now. The other children have all disappeared. Sister Isidore and her companion Sisters of Mercy have retreated to their convent. No one waits to make sure all children are picked up as eventually they always are and what could be a safer place to wait than the church steps? Besides, these two have each other: a girl who's eight going on nine, in a well-constructed homemade dress, her hair flat against her round, freckled face and her slightly taller brother, just past his tenth birthday, his features perfectly symmetrical from his proud forehead through his delicately chiseled nose right down to the dimple in the middle of his chin.

"Maybe Daddy's at the drugstore," Clement says. "We could walk to meet him."

"Yes, let's." I match his stride down the sidewalk, trusting him to know the way.

We keep our eyes peeled for the Kaiser-Frazer, which we don't see all the way down to Main Street, where to our left stretch familiar shops — Max Cutts's haberdashery, for instance, where the owner strokes the article of clothing a shopper is trying on, saying "Veddy fine ma-tid-dee-al" and offers a discount every time. Daddy can do a wicked imitation of Max Cutts. Farther along is the location of the florist shop which came with the greenhouse business and has been sold. Straight across at this end of Main Street is Rexall Drug. Perhaps Daddy has stopped inside there to buy Alka Selzer or Milk of Magnesia and has gotten to talking with the pharmacist, so that if we walk in he'll be delighted that we've saved him the time of driving all the way up to St. Mary's.

But Daddy isn't at the Rexall Drug, and the pharmacist, who greets us as mildly and pleasantly as though we were bona fide paying customers, hasn't seen him.

Daddy's been taken away, but we have no way of knowing that, and although he has been taken away from us once before, when I was two, I lack the imagination to think that such a thing could happen again. That first time we had been living near Augusta in a farmhouse with the romantic name of Ledgemere. As state treasurer, my father had gone to Florida for a conference and was returning by train when he went berserk and was taken off the train and committed to St. Elizabeth's Hospital in Washington, DC., where Ezra Pound, the poet and suspected traitor, was a fellow patient. That evening, two policemen came to the door at Ledgemere to give my mother the news. Alone, pregnant, and with three young children, she brought nine-year-old Tommy into her bed that night and held onto him to keep from shaking. The next day — she will tell me years later — she was "all right" and went about making plans to get us all back to Houlton.

During the year Daddy was gone, Mumma, Clement and I lived with my Vose grandparents on Watson Avenue in Houlton, Tommy with my McGillicuddy grandparents across town. The Watson Avenue house was a three-story semi-detached that smelled of lilies of the valley by the front porch and pickling spices by the back. Not a proper avenue despite its name, the street was one block long with generous sidewalks for the many children to play on. Like all children of the time, Clement and I were sent outside daily unless the weather was truly foul. On warm summer days, I had a penchant for sitting in mud puddles, and my patient mother sometimes changed me several times in the course of a day. One day Uncle Paul drove up and unloaded a red bicycle for Clement, which he got on and pedaled furiously, letting me stand on the back. We kids skinned ourselves frequently on the sidewalk and went about throughout the summer with scabby knees.

Whenever he had to use the car to run errands or tend to business, Grampa would call to Clement and me and "in two shakes of a lamb's tail" we were in the front bench seat next to him. It was Grampa's way of providing relief to my pregnant mother and my high-strung Nana. Having come of age in horse and buggy days, Grampa talked to the car as though it were a sentient being, exclaiming *Get along there* when he stepped on the gas and *Whoa back, Nelly* when he applied the brakes.

Inside the house, Clement and I regularly ignored the injunction not to climb up the stairs from the first floor to the second on the outside of the banister. One day I fell from the second floor to the first and was taken to the doctor to have my upper lip clipped together. Back home, I felt restored enough to drink cocoa through the clip. Another day, in the basement, after being warned by Grampa not to come too near the hot water hose he was filling the washing machine with, I got sprayed under my chin. I remember my Uncle Tom running up the stairs with me in his arms. That time the doctor said I'd eventually need plastic surgery because the scarred skin wouldn't stretch as I grew. I still have the scar but surgery was never needed. One afternoon our neighbor Mrs. Green phoned the house from Greens' Clothing Store, her place of business, to say that she could see me walking by myself along Main Street. Uncle Tom drove down to retrieve me.

Uncle Tom and Uncle Clem had bedrooms on the top floor of my grandparents' house. Uncle Clem had been wounded in the Battle of the Bulge and wore a cast on one leg. In homage, Clement and I stumped around the house with bread wrappers on our legs. Uncle Tom had a beautiful, sweet girlfriend, later my aunt, whom Clement and I called by her full name, "Mary Rush." Sometimes she came to Sunday dinner. "Look at me, Mary Rush," I'd say. "Look at me!" And she would. Nana served finnan haddie with duck sauce and mashed potatoes and peas and homemade pickles. She was known to be fussy — *I don't know as I approve* being an expression of hers. She wouldn't let me play with the porcelain dolls she kept on a high shelf in the living room — dolls I thought much more appropriate for a little girl's use than a grandmother's and, besides, she never did take them down and play with them herself. And yet, the day I placed each of a pair of new shoes on either side of my dinner plate, she let them stay — and even more to her credit, I later came to appreciate, she took the little remnant of our family into her home.

On Watson Avenue, Clement was my constant, my nearest and dearest, companion, and although I saw him as my brother and if offered a treat by a neighbor would ask for another to carry home to "my boy," I was confused about just how this big boy Tommy, who biked over to see my mother and received her undivided attention, was related to us. I did remember who Daddy was and that he would be coming home someday. When that day came, a car pulled into the driveway on Watson Avenue and two men stepped out. To my everlasting mortification, I cried "Daddy, Daddy" and ran to Uncle George. Since that time our family, now including Charlie — whom I believed my mother had fetched home from the hospital in her new pocketbook — has been reconstituted, and I know very well how all of us are connected and am convinced of our indissolubility. In Patten, Daddy wore suits and went to work each weekday and half of Saturday. Now he wears old clothes and a tan canvas hat with a rim all the way around with a green plastic insert above the eyes, and goes down the hill to the greenhouse just about every day. Whereas Clement may have glimpsed behind Daddy's mask and Tommy is this very day in the tragic reversal of an adolescent playing the adult with an unhinged parent, to me, Daddy is Daddy and nothing is amiss.

I think it was only the evening before — or possibly the evening before that — that Mumma and Daddy and Charlie and I knelt in the field to cover seedlings with cellophane cones against a forecasted frost. Mumma didn't ordinarily help with the work of the greenhouse. She had all she could do to keep up with cooking, cleaning, washing and ironing, but that night she worked outside — cheerfully, if memory serves. We were all four of us happy.

But sometime today between the time Clement and I left for Sunday School and now, our father has been taken away. Alerted to Dad's crumbling sanity, Uncle Paul has driven down from Houlton to help out. I will find out later that Dad had signed himself into and out of a mental hospital in Portland — more than once, I believe. But not having been cured and unwilling to return, he found matters taken out of his hands. Maybe there was no big scene. Or maybe "the authorities" were included — as they will be at a heart-stopping episode Clem and I will witness twenty years hence. Maybe Dad tore his hair and rent his clothes and raved like an Old Testament prophet. Maybe there was a doctor brandishing a syringe so that Dad, overcome, numbly agreed to ride the eighty or so miles to the Maine State Mental Hospital in Augusta. This time he won't be signing himself out. This time he's been committed.

The pharmacist doesn't object to an eight-going-on-nine-year-old and a ten-year-old hanging around his store unescorted and without funds. Clement and I spin lazily on the stools at the marble and oak soda fountain. We inventory the packages of nickel candy bars, Bazooka Bubble Gum and Smith Brothers

Cough Drops displayed by the cash register at child's-eye level. We roam the aisles, glancing at racks of newspapers and magazines and at shelves of surgical supplies and oddments, the familiar minty, medicinal air reassuring us, falsely, that all is well and that Daddy will soon be along.

When he doesn't come — and Daddy, who is often late, has never been this late — we decide we'd better meet him further along on the way. The pharmacist bids us a bland, indifferent goodbye.

Outside we turn left onto the approach to the Carlton Bridge — always "the Carlton Bridge," never merely "the bridge" to Daddy. By the water to our right is the Bath Iron Works, a shipbuilding yard. Once, our family attended the christening of a new ship, the sort of occasion Daddy loves — and loves for his kids to see. A Naval officer in uniform stood by a pretty woman, who broke a bottle of champagne over the bow. She was all dressed up, and we, too, although only a part of the crowd, were dressed in our best clothes. The iron works is Bath's major industry and Daddy, with a newcomer's enthusiasm, always speaks of it with pride. I somehow have mixed it up with the Iron Curtain, about which I know very little but which I greatly fear. In a recurrent dream, my recently deceased Nana Vose is trapped behind the Iron Curtain, which has situated itself flush with the Carlton Bridge in the yard of the Bath Iron Works.

The two-lane Carlton Bridge, the nondescript color of the river on a bleak day, stretches for a half mile over the Kennebec River. Once, Tommy and some high school classmates were walking across this bridge when they spotted fire coming from below the two lift towers that rise up in the middle. They ran off the bridge, found a phone booth and called the Bath Fire Department, which referred them to the Woolwich Fire Department, which they called only to be referred back to the Bath Fire Department. The fire eventually played itself out without professional intervention, which was a good thing, or Clement and I would not find ourselves walking single file close to the rail this late Sunday afternoon, talking companionably while keeping an eye out for the Kaiser-Frazer.

Fortunately, at the towers the roadway doesn't rear up to allow for a tall ship to pass, and so we hurry by and don't stop until we are on the Woolwich half of the bridge. Then we pause to lean over the rail and gaze at the water, its deceptively gentle edges bordering a swift current. You could lose your mind looking at the river from the bridge's woozy height. You could go mad, clamber to the top of the rail and jump. I turn away from the water and look towards the Woolwich side. No Daddy yet. We start walking again.

Woolwich heads a peninsula in tiny, watery, rocky, pine tree-studded Sagadahoc County, where the mighty Androscoggin, filthy with paper mill waste, and the equally befouled Kennebec meet headlong to commingle with several smaller rivers in Merrymeeting Bay. We walk past the Reid State Park sign — take that right, in a car, and in twenty minutes or half an hour you are at a long wide strip of sandy beach looking out into the Atlantic Ocean. Daddy has driven us there once or twice and always means to go again soon. Once, when we were about to dash into the waves, an older woman cautioned my parents that there was a strong undertow that day — " undertow," a new word to all of us and one Daddy savored, utilizing it over and over during the next few days.

Past a turn in the road is the Carlton Inn, where our family stayed one week the summer before we moved into our new home. We sat with other guests in the wooden rockers on the front porch of that big old Victorian, talking and watching the cars go by — "living by the side of the road and being a friend to man." Only this is Route One and the drivers go too fast and with too much purpose to stop and talk to anyone sitting on a porch.

The sparse traffic is fast for pedestrians, too, and Clement and I are careful to keep to the gravel shoulder. The road dips to a long low bridge crossing a marshy field that floods at high tide and provides pasture for cows at ebb. By this time, it seems that we may have to walk all the way home. Unlike Hansel and Gretel, we know the way. Also unlike that brother and sister, we don't have an evil stepmother but rather our own sweet, dependable, hard-of-hearing Mumma who reads fairy tales and other children's stories to us in hushed dramatic tones. Nor would our Daddy cave in to demands to abandon us; nor, as far as we know, is there a wicked witch in our family story. Nevertheless, abroad in the world, we two are Hansel and Gretel. We don't fight or argue or even quibble. Everything depends upon unity.

"Let's see if Daddy's at Larry's," Clement says.

Even though Daddy's car isn't standing on the gravel apron of Larry's, the small grocery story our family often stops at after Mass, we turn off the highway and mount the wooden steps. We're tired. I'm wandering in an aisle of canned goods when a man goes down on one knee before me and gives me a big smile. It's Uncle Paul! Someone, not Daddy or Tommy, has remembered to come for us. How did he find us here? It doesn't matter. Clement and I have been picked up. And Daddy, we discover, is gone.

2

The Next Day

Whatever domestic drama played out while Clement and I were at Sunday School, there is no trace of it once we arrive home. Nor do Uncle Paul and Mumma seem concerned that Clement and I spent the latter part of the afternoon making our way toward home on our own. Tommy, too, though the events of the afternoon cast a long shadow over his life, shows no sign of strain. My brother Charles retains no memory of the day. Perhaps he was sent down the hill to the Barley Neck Road to spend the afternoon at the home of Mrs. Swift, a grandmotherly woman complete with gray bun who dotes on him and whom he calls plain "Swift." Mumma explains calmly that Daddy has had a "nervous breakdown" and been taken to the Maine State Mental Hospital in Augusta.

"Nervous breakdown" will suffice for an explanation until the summer before Clem's sophomore year at the University of Maine. Mum and I are sitting with him at our dining room table in Houlton as he fills out a scholarship form when he looks up at her and says, "It asks if anyone in my family has suffered from mental illness. I put down Dad."

It's after supper and Mum's knitting. "That's right."

"It asks what he had."

"Manic depression." She sounds as calm as though she were saying, "Knit one, purl two."

"I thought so," Clem says quietly, and in his fine hand he writes down the official diagnosis. A year or two later, filling out a form at the U of M that asks for his father's occupation — by that time Dad was working in the office of Uncle Paul's appliance store — Clem writes "poet."

The morning after Daddy is taken to the hospital Uncle Paul kneels in the living room at the maple coffee table which with its two matching chairs are what remains to us of the florist shop in Bath. He blesses himself, folds his hands together and lowers his head. I have never seen my parents kneeling in prayer except in church. Mumma goes about her Monday morning routine. Odd though it is to see my uncle in this posture, it would be alarmingly out of character if Mumma joined him. (Do I catch her smiling to herself? Is she amused by him? Embarrassed?)

One by one, according to what each of us wants, Mumma prepares breakfast — oatmeal or Kix or poached egg on toast — or, a favorite, poached-egg-on-toast-without-any-toast. In between this short-order cooking — each of us, the same as all mornings, catered to like an only child — she makes lunches for Clement and me, the same menu we've had the whole time we've lived in Woolwich. Once, she asked if I wanted something different, and I expressed a desire for "sandwich spread," a concoction of mostly relish and mayonnaise I'd seen a classmate eat. Mumma said neither yea nor nay but never gives us sandwich spread. She cuts slices from one of the loaves of bread she bakes weekly and spreads peanut butter and jelly onto two sets of sandwiches, which she wraps in waxed paper with a special fold she read about in a ladies magazine and that she claims is done in drugstores, although I have never seen such a fold anywhere else — or known of a drugstore that sells sandwiches. We each get two homemade oatmeal and raisin cookies and a thermos of milk. The leftover breakfast cereal Mumma spoons into a dish and places on the back step. Our two mother cats, mousers who earn their keep by patrolling the greenhouse, know to come to the door to be fed but don't expect to be let inside. Although they despise oatmeal, they eat their way through it to get to the morsels of meat or canned cat food clever Mumma has buried underneath.

"Around and round the mulberry bush the monkey chased the weasel. The monkey thought it was all in fun. POP goes the weasel. POP. POP. POP." Mumma pops Charlie's striped jersey over his head, pops an arm through each armhole, lifts his corduroys one leg then the

other over his feet and up to his waist. At five going on six, he's old enough to dress himself, but if she waited for that to happen he might stay in his pajamas all day. I'm busy setting up all my dolls, each named for a cousin, in various spots around the living room. Ann I prop up on one end of the couch, Maureen, with her dark curly hair, on the other, Baby Sally wrapped in a blanket between them. And so on...

Clement and I carry our flat metal lunch boxes to the corner of the Barley Neck Road to wait for the school bus. Tommy has already left for Morse High School in Bath — where he can purchase a school lunch for twenty-five cents, less than what it would cost, Mumma says, for her to make him one. Charlie, who when school started in September said of Clement and me, "Those meanies go off and leave me here all alone," will spend the day climbing the compost pile behind the greenhouse to gather rogue marigolds (when Mumma cuts his fingernails, he reminds her to leave long the one he uses for snipping flowers), going down the hill to munch cookies in Swift's kitchen, eating lunch with Mumma and Uncle Paul. By mid-afternoon he will be sitting under a pine tree on the cliff above Route One waiting for the school bus to return. Every once in a while during the day, Mumma will open the back door and call to him, and every once in a great while instead of answering he'll hide behind a bush or tree or rock from which he can peek out to observe her growing consternation. (She hasn't lost Charlie yet, but as an old woman she will have recurrent dreams of his being a little boy and she not able to find him.) It's almost like an ordinary day. Except that Daddy is gone and no one seems to know when he will return.

In winter, we waited in the dark for the bus, but for some weeks now the sun has preceded us. The driver is a Mr. Basset, whom these rough, rural children refer to behind his back as "Mr. Bastard." Some of these same roughs greet Clement and me as we climb on board with a catcall fashioned from our unusual last name. We dislike this treatment but feel we have no choice but to swallow our anger and complain to no one — the ambiance of the bus as savage as the wilderness through which Hansel and Gretel

14

wandered. Mr. Basset, a lumpy, swarthy man with the jowls of the type of hound that shares his name, lets the children's conversations — consisting largely of taunts and insults — rise to a certain level before he roars out an order to "shut up." We cease and desist briefly, and then the noise level rises once again and again and again until finally Mr. Basset pulls over to the side of the road, turns to face us, jowls shaking, eyes popping, and lets loose a string of obscenities, which, finally, cows even the most willful among us, and the remainder of the ride to Central School is in silence.

The product of a mid-century, statewide push to consolidate scattered neighborhood schools, Central School has been in operation for less than two years. In September of the year before, Clement and I briefly attended the Barley Neck School. Each morning we walked down the road to the small white wood-framed building with pointed roof that stood above the road on an outcropping of ledge. It was a two-room school, grades one to four to the left of the entrance, five to eight to the right. While I had several classmates, Clement was the only student in third grade. During morning and afternoon recess, we children played tag under the trees and King of the Mountain on the boulders. One day some big girls from across the hall got permission to take me across the road to the pine grove where they had constructed a lean-to against the roots of a fallen tree. At noon, Clement and I walked home to eat lunch with Mumma, Daddy and Charlie. Before winter set in, the new school was at last ready with a classroom for each of grades one through four. (As for grades five through eight and the friendly Barley Neck big girls, the earth might as well have opened up and swallowed them, and by the time the planned fifth through eighth grade addition came about, those particular big girls would be studying home economics or steno or The Gallic Wars at Morse High School in Bath.)

After the tumult of the bus ride, the calm orderliness of Central School is a relief, and whatever horrid behavior of both children and adult prevails in the one place is absent in the other. I am in a room only with other third graders, and although certain names are duplicated — two boys have names so similar that they are always addressed as either Robert E. Merrill or Robert Merrill Jr. — I am the only Barbara. My teacher is Mrs. Scott. She's not the equal in anyone's eyes of the dearly beloved second grade teacher Mrs. Hopkins — whom we children call "Miz Hawkins" — but, from her desk where she sits sucking on purple lozenges, she runs a happy, constructive classroom. The window sills display the products of our papier-mache project. We brought newspaper from home, tore it into shreds, soaked it, squished and squeezed soggy lumps of it into animal shapes, let the sculptures dry — Mrs. Scott testing them with her fingertips each morning while, in eager anticipation, we awaited her verdict — then painted them. Mine is a black Scottie dog, which I take home at the end of the year to sit atop my dresser until I'm grown up.

Another project consisted of acting out stories in the Reader. Having been put in charge of a small group, I gathered up two brown paper shopping bags of clothes and other props one morning at home and staggered to our bus stop. Clement, unwilling to be associated with such vagabond behavior, refused to help out, even on the way back home when the bags were beginning to split. My group's skit, if I remember correctly, was a success.

Now, for several weeks, my reading group has halted our progress in the Reader to let the other groups catch up. In our daily circle, we read instead from *Smiling Hill Farm*, the saga of a pioneer family: a father, a mother, a young bachelor uncle and four children, in this case two boys and two girls. The Wayne family leaves their birthplace and their relatives to travel by covered wagon through the wilderness to where they build a new home high on a hill. First, like the Barley Neck girls, they live in a lean-to of sticks and boughs laid against the roots of a fallen tree. Like our family when our well runs dry, the Wayne children haul water in pails. They search out food, the way my grandfather Vose forages from spring through fall for dandelion greens on his own and other people's lawns, for fiddleheads, strawberries, raspberries and blackberries at the edges of ditches and fields, for

16

apples in abandoned orchards. Like every family of my acquaintance, the Waynes plant a vegetable garden. They make friends with other pioneer families, among whom Uncle William has found a bride, and today is the wedding. I love this family, the Waynes, whose life does not seem entirely remote from my own, and read, happily and loudly, when my turn comes around.

Across the hall in the fourth grade, Clement is not so happy. He always seems to be on the outs with his teacher. I want to stop her in the hallway and tell her that she should go easier on him, that at home my parents are careful not to cross him and that, most of the time, he doesn't fly off the handle the way he does in her classroom. Aware that grownups don't like being contradicted by children, I never get the nerve to speak up. Indeed, the following year I, myself, don't make out so well in her classroom.

At least, by now, Clement can read. In June of the year before, my mother and Mrs. Scott, trying to stay out of earshot of us kids, talked of having him repeat the grade because, although he loved to listen to Mumma reading aloud from a series of books that had belonged to her brothers — *Tom Swift and His Airship, Tom Swift and His Talking Pictures, Tom Swift in the Caves of Ice* et cetera — he himself couldn't manage even the simplest Dick and Janes. In the end, the adults decided to promote him so as to avoid the humility of being in the same class as his younger sister. And then, amazingly, when September came around, Clement could read anything put in front of him. His answer to how he had achieved this milestone? Comic books. Mumma had seen him plowing through Tommy's sizable collection but assumed he was only looking at the pictures. Although he's now a reader, the best part of school for him is recess.

We spend recess in the yard. Unlike the Barley Neck Road School, which evoked the homey feel of Norman Rockwell and fit as flowingly into its environment as anything constructed by Frank Lloyd Wright, Central School looks like an oversized, flat-roofed, nicely maintained chicken coop plopped down on a wide, flat bed of gravel. Beyond the gravel lie a heavy-duty swing set and

17

a field of grass. The wide-open space and the increased number of participants evoke different kinds of games in the children. A favorite is crack the whip. My classmate Gershwin Trot is the whip. Gershwin is bigger and older than anyone else in third grade. Although he can't read, which might explain why he is in the same class as his younger sister Beatrice, he's fearsome at cracking the whip. The longer the whip, the more fiercely the last two or three children are spun and, released, go flying off into the air to land at some distance on their hands and knees. In the grass if they're fortunate, in the gravel if not.

The swings are equally hazardous. When I pump I go high enough to feel a jerk when the arc hits its acme and reverses. If Gershwin or some other burly boy pushes me, I fear the swing might make a full circle and come back down without me on it. Either way, I do like to swing and to swing hard. Just moseying back and forth makes me feel sick to my stomach.

This day — and for many days following — while I engage in all the routines of school, a part of my mind is always with Daddy. I wonder where exactly he is. Maine State Mental Hospital in Augusta, I know, but what would such a place look like and how does Daddy fit into it? What is he doing? When will he come back to us? Is he still himself?

At three o'clock we leave the calm of Central School for the hurly burly of the yellow school bus. Clement and I sit together, my classmate Chrystal and her older sister Donna in the seats directly in front of us. Close to our stop, Donna suddenly kneels up on her seat to face us. "McGillicut-cut-cut," she chants, her face twisted into a sneer.

Wham! Clement slams her full in the face with the flat side of his lunchbox just as the bus stops. We stand and hurry out. There will be no repercussions for Clement. Mr. Bassett sees his job as driving the bus, not babysitting, and probably if Donna doesn't stop her wailing he'll shout for her to shut up until she does.

When Clement and I get home, Uncle Paul is still here. He's Daddy's brother, his younger brother, and we have seen a lot of him lately. During part of his visits, he's busy conferring earnestly

18

with Mumma and Daddy, but always he makes time for us kids. He sits me on his lap, calls me sweetheart, tells me that next to his daughter Maureen I am his favorite girl in the world. I know that my own parents care about me, but I'm not used to such demonstrativeness and sweet talk. I love it. I love him. Even though there's a niggling wish Maureen weren't paramount in his affections, I love her too, my much older, curly-haired cousin, whom I don't see very often or know very well but whom I know to be beautiful and good.

Uncle Paul is generous. Once when Clement lost a tooth he threw it into the pine needles outside our house — perhaps because he no longer believed in the tooth fairy, perhaps because he couldn't be bothered with the piddling amounts Mumma or Daddy would slip under his pillow, or perhaps because he sensed that even small amounts strained our finances. Shocked at the waste of a perfectly good source of revenue and the callous disregard for the tooth fairy and for the powers of imagination that made her possible, I reminded him that Uncle Paul was staying with us. Alert to new prospects, he enlisted me in searching the ground with him until we found the tooth.

Because Mumma keeps track of the preferences of regular guests at her table, she serves a supper that pleases Uncle Paul, who is allergic to or disdainful of certain foods. We kids like just about everything she cooks. We eat in the dining room where we have Sunday dinner, Uncle Paul presiding. He engages all of us in the conversation, jokes with us and laughs at our responses. "Got a match?" he says to Tommy at meal's end.

"No." Tommy, who knows this trick of getting a teenager to unthinkingly reveal a cigarette habit, laughs and turns his pockets out.

At bedtime, I make each of my dolls comfortable and choose one to sleep with. A one-bedroom bungalow with porches front and back, the Woolwich house is to the Patten house — which had a downstairs with an entrance hall and an upstairs with three bedrooms — what a sports car is to a sedan. We kids sleep in the unheated, glassed-in back porch. One evening during our first autumn in Woolwich our whole family stood here watching what was, according to Daddy, the hurricane of the century. Rain lashed the windows, lightning lit up the trees outside, and thunder rattled the whole house. It was what you might expect, Daddy said — sounding both awed and thrilled — living so close to the coast.

Charlie and I sleep in one double bed on one side of the porch, Tommy and Clement in another bed on the other side, our spaces delineated by bureaus. Tommy has strung his matchbook collection below the ceiling on the big boys' side. From his mirror hang the beanies — like the one Jughead of Archie Comics wears — which he's cut from discarded fedoras and decorated with campaign buttons that say things like "I like Ike." An outgrown chemistry set sits on his dresser, and in his top drawer are several harmonicas, sent away for from comic book advertisements and eventually to be passed along to us younger kids, each of us doggedly putting in time with the printed directions on what to do with fingers and mouth and none of us sufficiently musical to progress beyond a halting, squeaky rendition of "Little Brown Jug."

Mumma reads Charlie his favorite Little Golden book, *The Poky Little Puppy*. Five little puppies dig a hole under the fence. Then "down the road, over the bridge, across the green grass and up the hill" they go. At the top there are only four. The poky one is still at the bottom of the hill. He smells rice pudding. The four others race home, where, as punishment for digging a hole under the fence, their mother sends them to bed without dessert. By the time the poky little puppy arrives home, his siblings are asleep and he eats all the pudding himself. The next day the scenario repeats with chocolate custard for dessert. The third day it's strawberry shortcake, but this time there's a twist. The four little puppies impress their mother by sneaking out to fill in the hole and are rewarded with dessert while the poky little puppy has to squeeze between the fence boards and arrives far behind. "What a pity you're so poky," the mother says. "Now the strawberry shortcake is all gone." The poky little puppy goes to bed hungry and feeling "very sorry for himself." Charlie never tires of this story about the ups and downs of not sticking with the pack.

After Charlie's asleep, Mumma sits on my side of the bed to recite with me the prayers I already know and to teach me a new one. I'm learning the "Hail, Holy Queen." When we come to the part which goes, "Oh clement, oh loving, oh sweet Virgin Mary," Clement suddenly appears from his side of the porch, grinning. (I have been rather surprised to learn that clement means kind.) After he goes back to his own bed, Mumma and I continue talking. Clasping Ann — or Maureen or Baby Sally — to my chest, I come up with new topics one after the other in order to hold her there. This first day after Daddy's been taken away seems almost like an ordinary day.

Except that after Daddy's taken away, things don't seem completely ordinary for a very long time.

I hug my doll and my left thumb finds its way into my mouth — a habit I follow throughout childhood. Mum will tell me years later that she was proud of weaning me from the bottle at a year but suffered regrets when I replaced the bottle with my thumb. She doesn't chide me about it, but Daddy from time to time has taken an interest in breaking me of the habit. The latest scheme was painting my thumb at bedtime with a noxious liquid produced and sold for the purpose of thwarting thumb sucking. Daddy was so gleeful about the plan that I didn't mind much and that night I fell asleep without the benefit of my thumb. When I awoke in the morning, however, and Daddy examined my hand, we found that in my sleep I'd sucked my thumb clean. Daddy continued the experiment either until the bottle ran dry or until something else took up his interest, and what I learned was to keep my thumb-sucking as private as possible.

3

The Days Immediately Following

Uncle Paul leaves a day or two after Daddy was taken away, and Uncle George, another of my father's brothers, comes. He's not as charming as Uncle Paul nor as handsome, but like all my father's siblings he enjoys children and pays attention to us. His nickname for me is "Barbara Claire with the Light Brown Hair." Once when we lived in Patten, a big girl visiting across the street suggested to some of us younger children that we all say our first and middle names. When it was my turn I proudly said, "Barbara Claire with the Light Brown Hair."

"'Light Brown Hair' isn't part of your name!" the big girl said.

"Oh, yes it is," I said, smugly, and I walked her across the street to our kitchen to prove my assertion. It was when Mumma and the big girl exchanged smiles over my head that I realized how wrong I was.

Uncle George still calls me Barbara-Claire-with-the-Light-Brown-Hair and I love him for it. Perhaps because he and Aunt Celia have no children of their own or perhaps because of an innate sense of caution, Uncle George sees many dangers in our environment. He expresses particular worry about the elevator Tommy has strung up in a pine tree not far from the house.

Tommy will grow up to get a degree in engineering, and his talents for building and for investigation and invention have already manifested themselves. During each of the three springs we lived in Patten, he built a shack using castoffs from a nearby lumberyard and each fall he set fire to the structure and let it burn to the ground. In Woolwich he experiments with the cats, climbing high into a pine with a cat under his arms and dropping it upside down. Then he drops the cat lower and lower to determine how much space it needs to twist around and land on its feet. (The two mother cats were so fierce that, I think now, it must have been one of their equally feral but less powerful kittens that endured Tommy's experiments.)

The elevator he's built consists of two wooden crates connected with a rope slung over a branch of the tree and of such a length that when one box is on the ground the other is high in the air. Tommy utilizes us younger kids — and his own brawn — as weight and counterweight to raise and lower the device. Uncle George expresses the fear one of us younger kids, no doubt less nimble than a feral kitten, will get brained. Before he leaves, he makes Tommy dismantle the elevator.

When Uncle Clem and Aunt Dottie come for overnight, Mumma turns her bedroom over to them, — the best, most private room in the house, with the built-in maple bureau which Charlie slept atop in a mist-filled tent the time he had croup. Young and childless, Uncle Clem and Aunt Dottie sleep until nine o'clock in the morning while we kids hang around outside their door, cautioned by Mumma not to wake them, dying for them to get up. When they emerge, tousled and laughing before anyone has even said anything funny, we swamp them and they reward us with complete, playful attention.

A later visitor is my father's sister, Aunt Mary, and she stays longer, maybe a week. A decade younger than my father, pretty and unmarried, Aunt Mary works in Bangor, where she lives in a boarding house and drives her own car. The year Tommy stayed with our McGillicuddy grandparents in Houlton, Aunt Mary was still living at home, and the relationship they have resembles that of a big sister and a beloved, occasionally annoying, younger brother. Aunt Mary plays board games and cards with us. One day she takes Clement, Charlie and me to Reid State Park. While she suns herself on a towel and Clement and I splash in the waves nearby, Charlie, our own poky little puppy, wanders off down the beach and out of sight. Perhaps no one warned her that Charlie is impervious to rules and doesn't fear being on his own. He may, in fact, enjoy playing a sneaky game with the adult in charge. By the time Aunt Mary locates Charlie, in this instance oblivious to the alarm he has caused, she is so rattled she isn't much fun anymore. She swoops up towels and lunch boxes, cutting short our visit, all the while exclaiming at Charlie's what-me-worry attitude — something Clement and I are perfectly familiar with — and we drive back to Woolwich, we kids rather subdued by her frame of mind.

A happier occasion for Aunt Mary and Charlie occurs when the two of them spend a whole day together at our house. For lunch she fixes scrambled eggs — about the only thing she knows how to cook — and ever after it remains one of Charlie's favorite foods. That's the day someone drives Mumma and me to the Augusta State Mental Hospital to see Daddy.

Mumma and I mount the steps of a stone edifice big as a fortress and enter a wide cool entrance hall. A door opens, footsteps sound, and this time I'm enough older and such a small amount of time has passed that I cannot mistake who's approaching. "Daddy!" He looks like himself — a handsome, fit man of forty-three with a high forehead and the bright blue eyes and pink and white skin of the Irish. A natural blonde patch contrasts with his thick, wavy chestnut-brown pompadour; when my mother first laid eyes on him at a dance in their early twenties, she thought he must have used bleach to create the effect.

We go for a walk. The grounds of the Maine State Mental Hospital are as extensive as a park — or a cemetery without tombstones. We meander on paths through rolling lawns and trimmed hedges. Daddy points out flowering plants and budding trees as though Mumma and I were clients interested in hiring him to do some landscaping. He is subdued but not strangely so. He and Mumma talk comfortably, quietly, the way they did the night we capped the plants in our field.

Our ramble around the grounds brings us eventually back to the building where Daddy now lives. I am dying to go past the entrance hall. I want to see where he sleeps, where he eats. I want to know how he spends his days now that he is away from the greenhouse and from us. Try as I might, I cannot visualize what lies beyond the cool marble hall where we stand saying goodbye.

Afterwards, perhaps on the ride home, I state the opinion that Daddy seems perfectly okay. As an adult, I will find that my assessment got back to him and that he prized it, going so far as to look at his wallet-sized school picture of me whenever he sought reassurance that he would be well again. He will keep that picture, transferring it from wallet to wallet, for the rest of his life. Once, when Dad was at the First Communion Mass for one of my brother Tom's children, the priest talked to the little new communicants about the crosses, medals or scapulars they were wearing to commemorate the day. A sacramental, he explained, is any object that reminds us of God's love for us. Dad took out his wallet and showed the photo of me to Tom's wife Dina. When, absorbed in the task of raising my own young children, I first heard this story, I felt angry, angry that we kids had to be like grownups, my father the child. Madness struck me as a luxury indulged in at the expense of others. Now, I think of the terror he must have felt over losing his sanity to sickness, his memories to electric shock treatment and am glad of any saving role my picture played. After his death, Mum gave me the supple leather wallet that had conformed to his back pocket and in it the photo of a smiling, freckle-faced child who knows and loves her Daddy.

From the mantelpiece of one of the fireplaces in our living room, Clement steals a pack of Lucky Strikes out of the carton Uncle Paul once brought to Daddy. Except for the occasional cigar smoked in company, Daddy is not a smoker, and the open carton has lain barely used. Clement and I walk out into the woods behind our house — a wood bordered each of my childhood homes. This strip runs parallel to Route One from the Barley Neck Road on up where we dare not go nor hope to imagine. A path crosses a brook edged with frogs' eggs that look like spilt tapioca pudding and climbs to a boulder overhung by a tree from which Tommy has tied a rope that we swing from, like Tarzan, to land on our feet far below.

We sit on a log. The summer before, having become a precocious reader in second grade, I devoured *Tom Sawyer* and *Huckleberry Finn* among other volumes in our home library that dated back to my mother's own childhood. From time to time, like Tom and Huck, Clement and I come into the woods to seek relief from civilization and talk things through and smoke.

"Daddy went running down Main Street in Bath screaming in German." Clement produces matches, shakes out two cigarettes and hands me one.

I picture Daddy running past Max Cutts's and the defunct florist shop. Screaming. In German. Among Tommy's comics are ones about war. The bad guys are German or Japanese soldiers. I picture their wide-open snarls, their mouths webbed with spittle. "Daddy was talking German?"

Clement nods. "Perfect German….on Main Street, that's where they caught him." He scratches a match on a rock and lights his cigarette first, then mine.

"Who?"

"The cops. He put up a fight, but they caught him."

I picture cops chasing after Daddy, finally netting him like a fish or butterfly.

"If Daddy went around with other women…we can't hold it against him." Clement takes a puff.

"Other women?" *Besides Mumma?*

Clement exhales. "If he did, it wasn't his fault. He wasn't in his right mind."

I puff on my own cigarette and hold the smoke in my mouth. I picture the fancy women — I don't yet know the words "siren" or "sexpot" — in some of Tommy's more racy comic books. Only years later will it occur to me that Clement was drawing more from comics than from real life. For now, I have no choice but to believe him, but rather than integrate this alarming new information, I tuck it away on a very high shelf in my mind where it doesn't interfere with Daddy as I know him. I open my mouth and the smoke wafts out. Pine trees predominate in this woods and the floor beneath our feet is layered with dry brown needles.

The smell of resin overwhelms the smell of tobacco. A chipmunk scampers across the boulder and leaps to the Tarzan rope and then to the tree.

We kids will spend years trying to work out what happened to Dad, to Dad's mind. When I come across the writings of the psychologist and memoirist Kay Redfield Jamison, I will latch onto her term "mild mania." Is that the state Dad was in when he bought the greenhouse? I remember him coming back to Patten from trips to the coast, all pumped up about "saltwater farms" and other possible ventures. One day he sat me on his knee and described the new neighborhood we would be moving to. A girl my age — or possibly slightly older — would come down the sidewalk, he said, and ask me to play with her, ask me to be her friend. In our neighborhood in Patten there were only boys to play with. I knew that my parents were concerned that I didn't have girls my age nearby — although that would have changed within a year or so because there were girls up our street and across the road in a crosshatch of leafy streets where, before long, I would be old enough to walk to by myself. Perhaps in an effort to advance this agenda, just before we moved my mother planned a "tea party" for me and a couple of those little girls. The thought of a girl my age waiting for me in Woolwich to be my friend, however, was a delicious enticement, and when we arrived at the greenhouse I was disappointed to see that there was no sidewalk on either Route One or the Barley Neck Road; yet it was many days before I stopped looking for the little — or slightly bigger — girl who would be my friend.

Some years later I will ask my mother how she allowed herself to agree to Dad's overreaching plans that led to his breaking down a second time. "You don't know your father," she said, "He would get so enthusiastic he swept everyone else along. I made up my mind, after Woolwich, that I wouldn't go along again. When I got married, I thought the husband should be in charge. I had to let go of that idea."

His alluring fiction about the girl who would come down the sidewalk to be my friend gave me a touch of what it was like to be "swept along" by Dad's enthusiasm. Jamison says mild mania is the state in which many creative geniuses have achieved their finest works. Although at the time his enthusiasms seemed a normal part of his nature, perhaps Dad's last year in Patten was mildly abnormal. We took a trip to the coast. Was that normal? Daddy explained that we would save the money for our vacation by his giving my brothers home haircuts. He sent away for a barber kit, and every time he gave one of the boys a decidedly inexpert cut, he made a show of dropping the price of a haircut into a glass jar. Also, we would no longer buy soda. He bought several gallon jugs of an orange concentrate called Zarex, which we drank mixed with the proper amount of water, until we got sick of it, and consigned the remaining jugs to a shelf in the shed.

The trip was to Bar Harbor. One day there we took a sightseeing boat and listened to a guide with a microphone describe the estates we chugged past. Daddy was taken with the wealth and glamour these summer "cottages" represented. "How do you do, Mrs. Stotesbury?" he'd say from time to time afterwards, rolling around on his tongue the ritzy sounding name of one of Bar Harbor's dowagers. Did viewing the opulence of Bar Harbor set off in my father that pleasantly elevated, creative state known as mild mania and prompt him to throw over a workable life in Patten to risk a new venture for which neither he nor my mother were particularly well suited?

Probably Mum was reluctant to leave Patten. No doubt she harbored the memory — which electric shock treatment had erased from Dad's mind — of his first breakdown. And life was good. We were a comfortable day's round trip visit to our grandparents in Houlton, and she had made friends in our little town and belonged to a couple of women's groups. When Mumma had to take refreshments to a meeting, she made two kinds of sandwiches: cream cheese with minced olives and cream cheese with minced Maraschino cherries. Eschewing the loaves she baked for us each week and using instead a long loaf of store-bought white bread aptly labeled "sandwich bread," she would fill a large ceramic bowl with the four edges sliced off each sandwich, and we kids got to eat those chewy, cheesy crusts dotted with bits of olives and cherries. A few times she was the hostess. Daddy and Tommy would go out for the evening, perhaps to the movies, and we younger kids would be put to bed. Too excited to sleep, we would gather at the top of the stairs. We must have gotten noisy because, repeatedly, one of the clubwomen would sidle up the stairs and tell us to go to bed, which we would do, briefly, before emigrating to the top step once again because, after all, this woman was not our mother and we didn't have to do what she said. Mumma was oblivious to this naughtiness, but one meeting she was on high alert lest Tommy's pet chameleon, which had escaped earlier in the day and was in hiding, put in a sudden appearance on an armchair—or on a guest.

Before we moved, each of Mumma's women's groups presented her, coincidentally, with a pink and white glass candy dish, a matched set as it turned out. She placed them at either end of the mantelpiece in Patten and one day when we kids were horsing around one fell and smashed. Mumma threw her apron over her eyes and ran into the kitchen. Daddy was angry that we'd made Mumma cry, and we kids looked at each other in guilty silence. None of us cared about the dish itself; none of us could bear to see Mumma lose her composure. I followed her into the kitchen where she stood in the middle of the room, head bent, and thinking to make her feel better said, "You still have one left, Mumma." She only cried the harder.

4

Grampa to the Rescue

Grampa Vose, who now arrives to live with us, is, in his own way, as attentive to me as Daddy — perhaps more so because his is a steadier disposition. The summer before we moved to Woolwich, Mumma and Charlie and I stayed with Nana and Grampa on Watson Avenue while Tommy and Clement were with Daddy working at the greenhouse. Later Clem will say that even then Dad talked frighteningly big — the greenhouse was going to become a worldwide operation, fanciful ideas like that, ideas we will later know to call "grandiose."

Nana wasn't well the summer we spent on Watson Avenue, and Mumma went through old letters and prized possessions with her until the day Nana said she didn't want to look at anything more. Once, after she had been helped to the bathroom by an adult on either side, I looked into the un-flushed toilet, fascinated to see what looked like a bowlful of blood. The following summer I was visiting for a week in Easton with Uncle Tom and Aunt Mary when Aunt Mary told me that Nana had passed away in the night. "Passed away," I thought could mean either that she'd fainted or that she'd died. From Aunt Mary's solemn expression, I could see it meant the latter.

My grandparents didn't own the house on Watson Avenue or the house they had to move to during Nana's final illness. From the time he began sweeping out the Waterville office after school at the age of fourteen until he retired at sixty-five, Grampa had worked for a phone company that eventually became New England Telephone and Telegraph. Although his sister Nina graduated from Colby College and his crippled brother Harry attended for a year or two because their father feared that otherwise he'd never be able to earn a living, nobody suggested to my industrious, able-bodied grandfather that he continue his education beyond high school. As manager of the Caribou office, he came to understand that the lack of a degree prevented him from rising further, and so he made up his mind that all of his children would graduate from college, and they did. Late in his career, he managed the telephone company in Houlton, and when he retired he and Nana remained there, although why they didn't buy a house I don't know.

Now, in two shakes of a lamb's tail, Grampa disperses much of his belongings, makes a final rent payment and drives his Ford — with Grampa it was always a Ford in some shade of blue — down to Woolwich and moves in with us. He came from a time when the composition of a household needed to be fluid enough to accommodate orphaned kin, penniless spinster aunts, eccentric bachelor uncles, and aged grandparents. The youngest of nine, he was born on Election Day, 1880, and named Arthur Garfield for the Republican candidates. After his widowed oldest brother and three young children moved in, he became his mother's right-hand man — for all intents and purposes the oldest of four. Now tall and balding, although what hair he has is still mostly brown, Grampa is potbellied as a porker, outgoing as a puppy, industrious as a beaver. He erects a cot behind the piano. Whatever he does with his clothes and other possessions, they're stowed neatly out of the way. He lists our telephone number — 171 — in his name because along with a pension and his stock in AT&T, he has free phone service for life. A career manager, he sets about managing us. My mother inherited his even temperament and they get along easily. Charlie and I respond favorably to Grampa's attention. He absentmindedly calls me Ruth, my mother's younger sister's name, and without any sense of betrayal I slide easily into the role of Grampa's little girl.

With my older brothers, it isn't so easy. Behind his in-laws' backs, Daddy, a McGillicuddy chauvinist, used to make fun of their fussy ways. *I don't know as I approve*, he'd say, pulling a severe face, then laughing, signaling to us kids that Mumma's folks were fuddy-duddies. He'd keep up his teasing just short of the point where Mumma would lose her composure. Occasionally, he would go too far, and she would get up from the dinner table and run to the kitchen, her apron held to her face. Then Daddy would look abashed and we kids would be quiet until Mumma composed herself enough to return. Outright apologies didn't come naturally to Daddy, but he would make an effort to restrain himself and be nice to Mumma.

Now one of the fuddy-duddies is telling us what to do — pick up our clothes, clear the table and help with the dishes, put things back where we took them from, hold the screen door so it doesn't slam — and this state of affairs doesn't sit well with Tommy and Clement, who may feel that compliance would betray their surname. "Torrible" is the word Grampa uses for slovenly habits and "Yes, but" his way of saying no. Fortunately, for the sake of household peace and now that school is out, we kids spend many of the daylight hours outside.

The acre or so that comprises our property is a wonder of geological diversity. In the kitchen dooryard a fieldstone fireplace faces a picnic table where, in nice weather when we first lived here and Daddy could afford a crew, Mumma served many convivial midday dinners. A path slopes to the Barley Neck Road, and when our own well dries up, we kids trudge it carrying buckets of water from our neighbor Midge's artesian well. The bushes that grow on the steep descent next to that path could be cleared to make way for more cultivated shrubbery, were there time for beautification for its own sake. On the adjacent cliff, sheared through for Route One, Clement has explored the openings in the stacked ledge and discovered a series of caves, which Charlie and I follow him into until we can no longer see light and dare go no farther. We break off pieces of slate to use as chalkboards. Hunks of clay, mixed in with the slate and the same grey color, we mold into works of art.

Higgledy-piggledy across the lawn, boulders jut skyward and evergreens spread their boughs. Halfway down the slope on one side of the driveway, the grass ends abruptly at a sand pit, as much at home in this jumble as the slate, the clay, the evergreens and the boulders. The summer we visited and stayed at the Carlton Inn— the summer before we all moved in— the previous owners were still living in the house, and I remember the younger of that family's two little girls playing in the sand pile with nothing on besides her white underpants, a state of affairs Mumma would never have allowed.

On the other side of the driveway, just past the boards over our sorry well, the ground levels off at a field of wildflowers that Charlie calls his greenhouse. Beside and behind the actual greenhouse lies the garden, as large as a small field, in which grow the flowers and vegetables Daddy planted before he was taken away. The seedlings he and Mumma and Charlie and I covered against a frost now produce tomatoes, cukes and squash.

Scattered throughout our property are eruptions of gravel, from which Clement scoops up handfuls to let run through his fingers, searching for beauties. If Charlie or I find a pretty stone — most especially a pure white one — Clement persuades us to trade for one of his, maybe even two of his, and it is only when the prize is in his hands and his expression changes from studied indifference to delight that we realize we've been suckered. Other times I don't even need a trade to relinquish a stone because Clement has half convinced me that since he has more appreciation of beautiful objects than I have, he deserves them more. The especially beautiful stones Clement takes inside and puts into the shallow top drawer of his dresser, which he calls his "treasure drawer."

Also in the treasure drawer are marbles in a small felt bag with a drawstring. When it rains too hard for us to go outdoors, we set the cabinet of Mumma's Singer sewing machine against her bedroom wall as a backboard and play marbles. Clement's are the prettiest and he has most of the bigger ones, the shooters. In the interests of keeping the games going, he graciously lends some of his to Charlie and me. If it happens that either Charlie or I win a prized marble, Clement keeps the play up until he's won it back, and the games always end with the prettiest and biggest going back into his bag and into the treasure drawer.

Clement has opportunities for playmates besides Charlie and me, however. If he follows the woods path to where his classmate Johnny lives further north on Route One, then I'm left with Charlie and the pecking order shifts.

With his dark hair and handsome features, Charlie resembles our oldest brother. In fact, one day when the two of them were outside Max Cutts's in Bath, a woman said to Tommy, who has the height and lean features of an adult, "Your little boy looks just like you!" Unlike gregarious, highly active Tommy, however, Charlie has a dreamier, more self-contained nature. Throughout our Woolwich years, he has made the perfect playmate for me and much of the time I've been somewhat in charge of him. Over the last two years Mumma has tried to interest me in sewing and cooking and instituted several sessions on the piano bench to teach the rudiments of music, but I have resisted her efforts to relay the feminine arts, and rather than keep up the struggle, she's allowed the care of Charlie to be my main contribution to household order. (Perhaps to counter the notion that he's not his own person, however, he one day announces, "I know some things Barbara didn't tell me.")

I tell Charlie what his role is in my world of make-believe and what he is to do and say. "You're the father," I say. I pull on the sleeve of his striped jersey to lead him to the couch and place Baby Sally in his arms. "I'm the mother — 'Do you think Sally needs to see the doctor?' You say, 'Does she have a fever?'"

Charlie looks down at the doll in his arms, then up at me. He sticks out his lower lip and shoots a puff of breath straight up to feather his fine dark hair off his forehead. "Does she have a fever?"

And so the game continues entirely under my direction, giving great satisfaction to us both. Occasionally, Charlie fails to cooperate and I have to twist his ear, which ends things on a sour note. Other times, Clement asks to play too, and I hesitate because he won't put up with being fed lines or, for that matter, with playing house. He won't put up with being turned away either, and before I know it, he's lured Charlie into rambunctious behavior

34

that causes Mumma to say we can't play like that inside, and Charlie gladly follows Clement out, ending the game of house because Baby Sally and her sisters are for indoors. Last Christmas, Clement got hold of Maureen, my new doll, tied her rubber arms and legs together and used her to play catch with Charlie on the lawn. Everybody felt bad when Maureen crashed onto a rock and smashed her skull, but for me far worse than Maureen's smashup was Charlie's gleeful betrayal. When we lived in Patten and I had thought myself greatly outnumbered by the boys in my home and neighborhood, I used to say that when I grew up I wanted to have one hundred girls and one boy. Now, even Charlie, normally as docile as a little sister, is turning into a boy! Mumma sent away for a new head, and very quickly one came in the mail. Maureen's broken head screwed off and the new one screwed on, and in spite of a prominent ridge around her neck I love her just as much.

I would like a girl my age to play with. My school friends are just that, school friends, and there seems to be no way I can get together with them before September and the start of fourth grade. Beyond the greenhouse, across the brook and up a hill adjacent to our property lives a girl Charlie's age, and Debby is as willing as he to play for hours at a time with me in charge. Across Route One from the greenhouse is a farmhouse where a high school girl lives. One day last year, our whole family paid a visit to that family and when they were showing us around the place, Daddy squatted on a stool next to a cow in the barn, grasped her teats and caused milk to spurt into a pail. We kids all wanted to try, and Daddy gave each of us a turn on the stool and instructed us to pull rhythmically and with a little jerk to one side, but, try as we might, no milk came out. Daddy used to tell us about growing up on a farm where he did the milking morning and evening with Uncle George, who was a year younger. Daddy and George would squirt milk into the air for the barnyard cat to leap and catch in her mouth, but when Daddy would squirt George in the face, the younger brother would run crying to the house and Daddy would have to finish the milking by himself. Although it was couched as a cautionary tale — actions have consequences — Daddy always laughed at that part of the story.

During this pleasant neighborly visit, the teenage girl of the family put herself out to be nice to me, and I haven't lost hope of her as a playmate. It's never happened. This summer I make my way over there less and less because each time the mother tells me very kindly that her daughter is not at home or busy upstairs with housework or a project of some kind, offers me a cookie from a batch cooling on the kitchen counter and sees me to the door.

I know if I ask Mom for a nickel to spend at the Mom and Pop store she'll give it to me although I know, too, that money is tight and feel guilty the whole time I'm consuming the pack of Necco wafers or the joints of a Tootsie Roll. Money being tight is the reason that Mumma tries to stretch the time between perms — hard for her because she's not clever at curling her own hair, fine and straight like mine, and hopeless at attempting anything like a home perm.

And so I go home to read. One day the previous summer I was with Mumma and Tommy in the Bath Public Library when Mumma inquired from the librarian about my taking books out from the Children's Section. When Mumma heard that it would cost a dollar, she turned away without an argument.

And so I read what we have at home. I stretch out on the built-in couch in the corner of the living room between the front porch and one of the fireplaces. When he first arrived, Grampa presented me with my very own copy of *Smiling Hill Farm,* and once again I sink into the bosom of the idyllic Wayne family. Otherwise, most of our home library consists of the children's classics, such as *Treasure Island, Robinson Crusoe* and *Swiss Family Robinson*, that Mumma grew up with.

Like the Waynes, the Robinson family feels familiar. They explore the entire island, the way my brothers and I tramp the woods and streams behind our house. Like us, they build lean-tos and tree houses. The father, like Daddy before he was taken away, is usually close to home, planting, transplanting, weeding, watering, and when he goes exploring he includes his children —

one daughter in a family of mostly boys. He explains things and teaches the kids how to do the things he knows how to do — the way Daddy used to do.

The Robinson mother feels familiar as well. She cooks whatever possibly edible flora or fauna the father and children bring home. When we first moved to Woolwich we were at the dam swimming when my parents spied milkweed, recognizable by its seed pods bursting with fluff, and got into a lively discussion on how to boil away the toxins to make the plant edible. At that same dam in the spring alewives swimming upstream to spawn are so thick in the sluiceway that even a child can catch them barehanded. My thrifty mother has cooked them all kinds of ways until we can no longer stomach them no matter what she tries. The whole Robinson family, like us when Daddy was home, spend a lot of time together and depend greatly on each other.

Louisa May Alcott's books are also about family members relying on each other. In *Little Women*, as in my family, there are four children, only, in this case, all girls, girls who depend upon their wise, loving mother and long for the return of their absent father. I have great feeling for the plucky orphan Rose in *Rose in Bloom* and *Eight Cousins*, who, taken in by kindly relatives, joins an extended family of seven boys and has to learn how to get along with them. What appeals to me in all the Alcott books is the characters' concern for each other and the yearnings and frustrations of girlhood.

For more boyish fare, Tommy has given us younger kids free access to his comic book collection, good for reading and rereading. The really scary war comics display snarling Japs and Nazis, saliva strung through their teeth. *G.I. Joe* isn't scary because Joe spends his time playing games with children and giving them candy. I like that series almost as much as the *Little Lulu* one, which Tommy scorns, but sometimes accepts in a swap with the simple-minded fellow who clerks at the Mom & Pop store. It's about kids who live where there are sidewalks. Lulu is always meeting up with Sluggo, a little tough in a visored cap who struts around with his hands in his pockets, or one of the other kids in their gang— she is never pictured alone for long.

Very best of all are the Classics Comics. They tell some of the same stories we have in books: *Tom Sawyer, Huckleberry Finn, David Copperfield, Uncle Tom's Cabin.* In all these stories, orphaned or half-orphaned children — or dependent grownups — struggle and ultimately prevail in an inhospitable world. Always, there are kind adults who come to their rescue and shepherd them to maturity.

While I've been reading, Mumma has set up the ironing board in the dining area of our great big living room. Ironing comes after the heavy housework of the morning and before preparation for supper. She says it relaxes her. Often she hums as she works. If I ask, she'll tell me a story. I put down my book, get up off the couch and wander across the room to a dining room chair. "Tell me a story, Mumma. Please." With a thump, she rests the iron on the board and picks up the sprinkler to spray a shirt. Briefly, she looks off into the distance searching her memory. Then she picks up the iron, runs it over the shirt collar and begins.

Mumma was born in Houlton and grew up further north in Caribou in a house her parents owned. Although her mother always said they were poor, Mumma realized looking back that that wasn't true. Nana and Grampa had both grown up in Central Maine and that's where all Mumma's relatives lived. At Christmas time, they exchanged gifts via the mail. Her Uncle Tom always sent a large box of popped popcorn. In Caribou, dinner parties and even holidays were spent with families they weren't related to, and Mumma and her sister and brothers called some of the adults in the other families "aunt" and "uncle."

Next to Mumma in age was her sister Ruth. Like me, Ruth and her friend Doris loved dolls and Mumma didn't find them — Ruth, Doris or the dolls — very interesting to play with. For Christmas, Ruth and Doris went to the Five and Dime where each picked out the present for the other to give her. That seemed funny to Mumma, who thought the whole idea of a present was for it to be a surprise. Ruth didn't like to help out around the house and would shirk slicing bread, for instance, by claiming my mother could always do a better job. "Let Mary do it," she'd say.

Next came the two boys in the family, first Thomas and then Clement, named for my mother's beloved Uncle Clem, who was my Nana's brother and a newspaper man in Augusta. Also, all the time Mumma was growing up, Nana's bedridden mother lay in one of the upstairs bedrooms. One day, my Nana went into her mother's room and found the bed empty. Panicked, she searched the house and found her mother on the first floor. What had possessed the old lady? Mumma's Nana explained that she had grown tired of her room and wanted to see something different.

She really was an invalid, however, and after that one heroic venture never again came downstairs. She sat up in bed sorting socks, helping with the household sewing and mending, and relating family stories to her granddaughter Mary, my Mumma. She let it be known that when she died she wanted Mary to have her diamond ring. (After I'm grown up, Mum will have it made into a pinkie ring for me and I wear it to this day.) Mumma's Nana always wanted to be sure that the children had nice new clothing ready to wear to her funeral, which would be in Augusta where many relatives would gather.

When Mumma's Nana did die, my Nana had just given birth to Clement, a midlife baby that cost her her teeth, which slowed her recovery. So, only Mumma and her father accompanied the casket on the train to Augusta. Their stay was extended when my mother came down with the mumps. Meanwhile, back in Caribou, five-year-old Thomas caught whooping cough and the house was quarantined. Years later, my Uncle Tom said that when he was finally allowed to roam the house again, he found that his grandmother had been replaced by a baby.

Since Mumma's sister and brothers were all much younger, her playmates were neighborhood children her age. One was a self-assured little boy with the wonderful name of Parker Briggs, whom I picture as a well-dressed version of Sluggo. Mumma's friend Elvira was a blonde blue-eyed beauty who had no idea she was adopted although all the rest of Caribou, including the children, had heard the story her parents put out — and nobody believed — of finding her on their doorstep. In high school, the Swedish students who were bused in from the neighboring farm communities of Stockholm and New Sweden and who remained aloof from the Caribou students treated Elvira as one of their own, which, her Caribou friends concluded, she no doubt was.

"But, Mumma," I say. "Didn't Elvira get suspicious when the Swedish students were so nice to her?"

"No," Mumma says, running the iron over a handkerchief. "She'd always been made of and fussed over. That's the way she expected everyone to treat her. Besides, Elvira wasn't one to question things." When, Mumma says, the evening before her wedding, her parents sat her down and told her she was adopted, she was thunderstruck — and heartsick.

Elvira later adopted a daughter of her own, and once these two came to visit us in Woolwich. Like me, Elvira's daughter carried a doll around, but, unlike Ann, Maureen and Baby Sally, her doll, she informed us, was adopted.

Mumma tells me that one day when she was a student at Colby College, she took her watch into a jewelry shop in Waterville because it had stopped ticking. That's how she found out she was losing her hearing. Her Uncle Philip, a doctor, arranged for her to see specialists, but nothing could be done to stop the decline, which continued over the next decade. The cause was laid to either measles or mumps, severe cases of which my mother suffered rather late in childhood. With the mumps, she remembers lying in bed on her back, her swollen cheeks spread out on either side of the pillow.

(Possibly, however, neither mumps nor measles was responsible for the loss; possibly it was a Vose family trait. Mum's Uncle Tom — the popcorn giver — was so hard of hearing people had to shout and even then couldn't always get through to him. Her brother Tom will become hard of hearing in midlife, as will one of his sons, as will my brothers Clem and Charles.)

Mumma's hearing was at its worst when we lived in Patten. We kids — and Daddy, too — used to shout "Mumma, hey" to get her attention, and she would calmly reprove us. "My name is not Mumma Hey. Hay is for cows."

Now she has better hearing aids. Two batteries the size of sausages sit in a cloth bag in the cleavage of her bra and wires run to bulky instruments in her ears. With her aids removed — at night, for instance — she's practically deaf. Sometimes during the day she'll say, "If you kids don't quiet down, I'm going to turn you off," which she can do by reaching into her bra and twisting a dial. Once in a while, if we ask, she lets us kids try the instrument. I put the receiver into my ear. It sounds like a staticky radio that keeps shorting out. No wonder Mumma's ability to hear seems so touch and go. If the receiver loosens up, it emits a squeal too high-pitched for her to hear, and one of us kids has to grab her arm and point.

When Mumma graduated from Colby in 1929 at the age of 20, she took a teaching job in a small farm community near Caribou. After two years, her Colby chum Ethel told her she was burying herself out there in the country and urged her to come to Houlton, where, according to Ethel, there was plenty going on. Mumma took the train down, interviewed with the superintendent, and was hired to teach high school English.

Ethel's friend Celia went around with a fellow named George McGillicuddy, who had a brother named Joe, and she arranged for my parents to meet. Once she and my father started going together, my mother would invite him for Sunday dinner at Mrs. Donald's where she boarded. Another boarder was Evangeline Hart, the young, beautiful high school music teacher, who was as unworldly as Elvira had been. One Sunday during dinner — it was Daddy who once told this at our supper table, Mumma listening with amusement to a tale too risqué for her to relate — Evangeline breathlessly informed the table of her recent discovery, verified by witnessing a man urinate off the side of a moving train, that men were built differently from women.

For a couple of the summers when Mumma had an unpaid vacation from school, she and Celia and Ethel and Eleanor, another Colby chum, went down to Ogunquit, a beach resort, and

41

waited tables. In between serving breakfast and dinner, they were free to go to the beach, and Mumma has a picture of them posing flirtatiously in old-fashioned bathing suits. Another summer my mother and Eleanor sailed to Europe to take the Grand Tour. Listening to Mumma as she irons shirts and blouses and dresses and pants and sheets and tablecloths and everything else that she pushed through our wringer washer twice, hung on the clothesline (maybe also twice, depending on the weather) I marvel at the free and easy, friend-filled life she led before she married Daddy and had us kids.

When, four years after she moved to Houlton, she married my father, Mumma had to give up her teaching job. Because it was the Depression and there weren't enough jobs to go around, married women weren't allowed to teach, their husbands' incomes seen as sufficient. (In Mumma's case, I later come to understand, her teaching career was already doomed by her deteriorating hearing.) No longer living with her parents or in a college dorm or with Mrs. Donald, she had to manage a household. Mumma says she spent the whole first year of marriage learning to make pie crust.

Listening to Mumma's stories, reading, playing with my brothers, with my dolls, tramping through the woods, shinnying trees, walking to the bridge or dam under Tommy's supervision to swim (i.e. wade), the summer is passing by. My birthday has come and gone, and so I am nine. I suppose Mumma created a little ceremony of cake and candles and everyone singing, but I have no memory of it. The birthday I do remember is the day I turned seven. Our family was traveling from Houlton to Woolwich to stay at the Carlton Inn, and we stopped at a roadside restaurant for supper, at the end of which a waiter appeared with a whole pie with lighted candles, and he and my family and all the other diners sang "Happy Birthday." Afterwards, Daddy explained that he had requested a cake, but the restaurant only had pie, and in his inimical way of making a child feel special, Daddy declared that any little girl could get cake for her birthday, while I alone got pie! Mumma is Mumma and I know I can always count

42

on her, while Daddy is often busy with other concerns, but when he turns his full attention to me, I'm captivated.

It's like the time in Patten when we were preparing for the vacation, and Daddy put the matter to a vote and Bar Harbor won five to one, I having voted for Old Town, of which I had heard my friend Bobby speak — his grandmother lived there. When we crossed the bridge at Old Town, a light-manufacturing town far from the coast and certainly no tourist destination, Daddy took a second vote, and because he so cheerfully took me into account, I didn't mind losing. Although Daddy is in Augusta State Mental Hospital, he retains a big space in my heart and mind.

Raised as a Universalist and looking for fellowship, Grampa drives us to St. Mary's on Sunday mornings with certain expectations and is astounded that the congregation scatters after Mass without so much as a word to our family — except from Sister Isidore and from Father Maney, who, in spite of scolding adults from the pulpit as though they were children, goes out of his way to speak kindly to actual kids.

Back home, Grampa takes charge of Sunday dinner, just as he did the whole time he was raising his family to free up his wife — the former Florence Murphy — to take the children to Mass, delaying his own conversion to Catholicism until about the time I was born. (Once, in later years, Dad said Grampa converted only in order that he and Nana could be buried side by side. This, if true, sets him in several possible lights — opportunistic, pragmatic, romantic, transcendent, enlightened. Grampa's only objection to Catholicism, I'm told, was Hell, which he accepted when the priest giving instructions said that as a Catholic it was necessary to believe in Hell but not that anyone has actually ended up there.)

Although Sunday dinner consists of a roast, potatoes, vegetable and pie, Grampa's other meals can be quite unconventional. For breakfast, he might have a slice of apple pie left over from the night before with a hunk of cheddar cheese. He quotes the maxim, "Apple pie without any cheese is like a hug without a squeeze." Items that the rest of us would eat only hot, such as cooked dandelion greens — a "mess" of greens in Grampa's parlance — he slathers with mayonnaise and eats cold, refrigerator leftovers being an endless source of pleasure. He delights, in fact, in the entire food cycle from selecting seeds to gardening to cooking to a well-laid table to tasty leftovers.

From Daddy's garden, he harvests a bounty of huge summer squashes and with us kids along for the ride — *Get along there! Whoa back!* — drives into Bath to sell them to supermarkets. Smiling with satisfaction, he hands the cash over to Mumma. She doesn't tell him it barely covers the cost of growing the crop.

Periodically, Grampa sits down to the big typewriter on Daddy's desk, rolls in several sheets of onionskin separated by carbon paper, and with two fingers types out a letter with the heading, "Spuds Special," spuds being a reference to Aroostook County, potato country. We used to get one of the carbons in the mail before he came to live with us, and we know that it's a sprightly compilation of the doings of his children and grandchildren and a rather too detailed account of his own activities since the last "Spuds Special." Mumma used to read the newsletters to us at the supper table, along with any other family letters, ones from Aunt Ruth being most common. We were interested in anything touching on ourselves and slightly bored by everything else but, taking our cue from Daddy, who no doubt shared our feelings, we sat quietly and didn't interrupt. Now Grampa reads a copy to us kids, and it's more interesting because it's more about us and, also, we have a context for the stories he's telling about himself.

In his zeal to impose order and bring his grandchildren to heel — pick up after ourselves, help our mother, not let the screen door slam — Grampa finds Charlie and me good-naturedly noncompliant, Tommy and Clement sneakily defiant. "There's no need of it," Grampa says about each of our many transgressions. When, at one point in the summer, my older brothers ride back to Houlton with visiting McGillicuddys, peace settles on our reduced household. Then the boys seem to be getting along so well, Tommy at Nana and Grampa McGillicuddys', Clement at Uncle George and Aunt Celia's, that Mumma decides, when invitations are issued, to let them stay until the rest of us — surely that will soon include Daddy as well — join them. For we are selling the greenhouse.

5

Fourth Grade Begins

This fall Charlie starts first grade and becomes my new companion on the bus. I'm happy to be back with my old classmates, most especially dark-haired Judy and blonde Sandra, who become my best school friends. The work in fourth grade, however, is irksomely different from what I've encountered up to now. We spend what feels like most of the day filling out workbooks, and I, who can read almost anything that comes to hand, cannot distinguish among the short vowel sounds and have to erase so many times I make holes in the porous pages. I feel so cross and out of sorts that apparently one day I do something belligerent. Almost before I know it, I find myself sitting on a chair in the hall, the teacher having expelled me from the class. I don't care. I feel hard as nails, as Grampa might say, and wouldn't give anyone the satisfaction of showing emotion.

Then Mrs. Hopkins, my beloved second grade teacher, comes along, stops, looks down at me, says softly, "Oh, Barbara," and I burst into tears. I don't remember ever feeling so hard or horrid in second grade, and yet something about my behavior — perhaps it was talking too much — was sometimes a problem then, too. One day, Mrs. Hopkins told me that I must stay right next to her for the rest of the day, a punishment I gladly accepted. When a boy threw up and she had to fetch cleaning materials, I got to follow her into the boys' bathroom, the only room in the building I'd never been in before and one I'd been curious about. In Mrs. Hopkins's class, even if she expressed disapproval at my constant talking out of turn, I never felt cast out of her favor.

I do love to talk and this year I have the frequent and sublime privilege of talking at length to all four of the teachers at Central

School. During recesses and lunch, Mrs. Hopkins, Mrs. Scott, the first grade teacher whom I never had, and the fourth grade teacher whose name I've since forgotten, all stand inside the double doors of the school, leaning on their forearms and glancing through the plate glass at their charges. I come back into the building to use the bathroom, and as I'm about to go outside again, one of them asks how things are going at home. In the questioning that follows, I tell them everything I know about our situation. I talk until the bell rings and it's time for us to go back to the classroom. Although I don't have much new to add, the teachers never seem to tire of hearing me relate our story. I'm thrilled at the attention they give me, and at the same time am aware that they are trespassing and so when I go home I, who like to tell Mumma all about what happened at school, omit the teachers' grilling that I gladly submit to. Nor do I tell her that the teacher put me out into the hall.

In the best rural tradition, our nearest neighbors scattered along Route One and up the Barley Neck Road put themselves out to help Mumma. Business — possibly a visit to Daddy — sometimes takes Mumma away from us. Because of her hearing handicap she's never been a driver and so Grampa or someone has to take her anywhere she goes. One day, Charlie and I are left to spend the day at the home of the Werters, who have moved to our little Maine town from New Jersey. At the dinner table, husband and wife call each other "Mr." and "Mrs." "Please pass the salt, Mrs. Werter," Mr. Werter says.

"Here you go, Mr. Werter," Mrs. Werter says.

"We call each other Mr. and Mrs. Werter as a joke," Mrs. Werter explains, seeing the confusion on my face.

I get the joke. I don't say that what confuses me is that they pronounce "Werter" as "Whiter."

Daddy's broad wooden desk and office chair, where he sat evenings going over business, take up one corner of the huge living room. I sit in Daddy's chair at Daddy's desk. I open the drawer and take out a sheet of white stationery with green

47

McGillicuddy Florist, cead mile failte at the top. I take the cap off a ballpoint pen and write on the paper. It's wonderful, powerful, to be sitting in this chair, writing on this once sacrosanct paper, wonderful and terrible. I must have been given permission, or at least no one stops me. There is no more need for this stationery. I use it at will and add it, marked-up, to a clutch of discarded mail that I call my "business."

Charlie and I play greenhouse in the garden and field. Delicately, we squeeze the snapdragons to make their tiny mouths pop open and shut. We fashion little faces out of acorns — pull off the cap and set it aslant like a beret, use a pen to make eyes, nose and mouth, stick a matchstick into one corner of the mouth and *voila!* Like our little men, we too pretend to smoke — using twigs instead of real cigarettes.

Each Saturday, Aunt Celia requires Clement to write home before she gives him his allowance, and so the first of every week a letter arrives from him, and Mumma reads it aloud at the supper table the way she always has with letters from far-off relatives, one of which Clement has become. He sounds happy. We don't hear so regularly from Tommy.

After someone — Grampa, perhaps — provides Mumma with yards and yards of various material, her every spare minute goes into creating Christmas aprons for all the grandparents, aunts, uncles, and cousins, for it is a family tradition to gift each one, and Mumma doesn't want to come up short this year. That's a total of over thirty aprons: white broadcloth three-pocketed butcher ones for the men and boys, flowered chintz for the women and girls. It just about wears Mumma out, and even at nine years of age I don't think myself ever capable of such heroics — or is it foolish pride?

But, then, sewing is among the womanly arts that I eschew. It's hard enough that I have to stand still while Mumma kneels, pins in her mouth, to hem up a dress she's making for me. What apparel she doesn't make for me comes in boxes from Aunt Pauline and Aunt Dorothy at the beginning of each season. Last spring, Mumma lifted out a handsome pair of pants that had been Mary Alice's. "These would be nice for Clement," she said. "Don't tell him they came from a girl."

Of course, I do tell him, and after that he refuses to wear them and they become mine. Soon after, I stain them with pitch shinnying up a tree so that Mumma deems them no longer suitable to wear to school. Like St. Augustine in his childhood incident with the pear tree, I am ever after remorseful, for I know, even though my elders don't drum it in, that money is too tight for such selfish behavior.

Clement and Tommy are coming home for Christmas for sure, and if we're lucky so will Daddy. Grampa will spend the holidays with Uncle Tom and Aunt Mary and Baby Sally — the real baby Sally, not the doll — or with another of his children's households, Uncle Clem and Aunt Dottie or Aunt Ruth and Uncle Norman. Or maybe he will drive to Concord, New Hampshire, home of Aunt Nina, his doting older sister and widow of Uncle Philip, the physician. If Daddy gets permission to come home — for at Augusta State Mental Hospital he lives as much under supervision as I do at Central School — our family will be whole and intact unto ourselves.

In mid-twentieth century, denizens of the remote areas of New England have not yet learned from television to freely hug and kiss and say I love you, and so greetings and farewells would look awkward, even strained, to an outsider. (It's certainly TV that limbers everyone up in the area of expressing affection and other behaviors as well. Years later, my father will remark that after a lifetime of bathing sitting up, he has taken to lying down in the bathtub the way people on TV do.)

Our family is all together for Christmas. After initial awkwardness, we're as we always were — only different. Clement is different because he no longer tries to take Charlie away from me. One day Clement and I tell Charlie to stay by the phone in case Santa Claus calls. Then Clement and I run to the greenhouse, and Clement dials 171. He says he's Santa, and gullible Charlie lets himself be engaged in conversation. Then Clement asks if Charlie wants to talk to Mrs. Santa. No, Charlie does not. Clement wheedles but Charlie is adamant. Clement hands the phone to me anyway, and I prattle on, glad to enter a bit of pretense I'd been denied because no sooner had I heard of Santa than my older brothers assured me he didn't exist.

We three kids sit peacefully on the boulder closest to the house while Clement talks about Houlton, a wonderful place full of our McGillicuddy relatives. "Their doors are always open," he says. "Wherever you are in town, you can walk right in and sit down and if they're eating you can eat too." He explains what's different about living with Uncle George and Aunt Celia. For one thing, if there's a treat, he doesn't have to finish his quickly, for there are no other children to poach his share. "But I could learn to eat quickly again if I had to," he tells us. He says he's picked out a best friend for me — his classmate Peter's sister Ann, who's my age. During this vacation, Clement and I don't fight. (In fact, we will hardly ever even disagree again throughout the rest of our lives. In my sixties, I will wake up one morning with the dreadful feeling that, in spite of the fact that Clem and I no longer share life on a daily basis, if he were to die I wouldn't be able to go on living. The dread passes; I believe I would be able to live without him; I hope I won't have to.)

Tommy is different, too. The cherished oldest grandchild on each side of the family, named Thomas Arthur for both grandfathers and up to then a good student, he came and went in Houlton with the freedom of an adult and the mind of an adolescent, with the result that he is failing his classes.

Most different is Daddy. During the day, he follows Mumma around the house, plaintively, saying that he would like to have another child, a son that he would name after himself. "You've always said you never wanted to name a son Junior," Mumma says.

"I've changed my mind," Daddy says. These scenes are so striking that they will remain in my mind until I'm old enough to understand what lies behind them.

One thing is the same. Like every Christmas since I can remember, Tommy selects and cuts down the tree. We younger kids follow him into the woods, and he and Clement talk of the relative merits of several trees until we come upon the likeliest, which Tommy fells with his hatchet. He drags it home, we younger kids pulling on the back boughs to help it along. Mumma meets us at the door with a dubious look. Once again, the tree is higher than the ceiling and Tommy has to lop off the top before setting it up in its red and green metal stand. We all step back to view it. It is not the blue spruce or Norfolk pine of a Christmas tree farm but a humble native fir hacked from a Maine secondary forest, hedged in and deformed by bigger specimens. Ours has some handsome boughs but not evenly spaced; in fact, there are too many prominent bald spots to hide against the back wall. Belatedly, we kids realize we may have failed to meet Mumma's standard, and we turn our gaze anxiously, hopefully, to her as she struggles to control her emotions and accept graciously our poor offering. "It'll do just fine" she says, managing a weak smile, and Tommy sets about stringing the lights. She helps him hang the delicate colored balls and then we all apply tinsel. "Hang each strand," Tommy commands us younger kids. "Don't just throw it on in bunches."

I don't remember if Dad helped with the tree that year, but if he did he stood back and threw the tinsel on in bunches the way he always did. I do remember him in later years sitting reading in a chair next to the tree and every once in a while pinging one of the colored balls with his thumb and forefinger and every once in a great while a ball shattering, which he always greeted with a surprised laugh.

Christmas morning, my new doll and other presents pale in comparison to the greatest gift of all: Daddy. Wearing his plaid wool bathrobe, he sits in his office chair next to the tree, we kids at his feet watching him open his presents one by one.

One bright and sunny afternoon a few days later, I go with Daddy and Mumma on a walk down the Barley Neck Road. A ways past my old school on the opposite side of the road is a big white farmhouse lived in by a man who runs a filling station in Bath. When, on impulse, Mumma and Daddy pay a "dooryard call," the woman of the house invites us in. We sit in her living room, and my parents exchange small talk with her until she says something that startles them. "Oh, I thought you knew," she says. "I thought that's why you stopped in." On Christmas day, her husband, she tells us, absconded with the secretary of the filling station. "Ran off to Florida."

My parents say how sorry they are and that they'd never have stopped in, had they known.

"Oh, but I'm glad you did," she says, and I see that she really means it. Like all the neighbors, she knows of our troubles and now we know hers, and for a few minutes on this afternoon of Christmas week she isn't alone in her sorrow. She doesn't act angry; she doesn't rail against her husband or the secretary; she minds her manners and is a gracious hostess, but I think and continue to feel *how awful* even though after a few weeks, her husband returns home, says he's sorry and she takes him back.

And Mumma and Daddy and I, as we make our way back home, are strangely heartened by thinking about someone else's troubles, troubles as undeserved as our own but somehow more terrible because that husband ran away from his wife, *with another woman,* whereas Daddy hasn't taken up with anyone else and would give anything to stay home with us instead of going back to the Augusta State Mental Hospital. He doesn't go into detail about the hospital but he says several times that it's worse than prison because a prisoner knows when his sentence will end but with a mental patient the key has been thrown away. Somehow, I understand that besides the doctors at the hospital, some of our uncles and maybe even Mumma are the possessors of that key.

Daddy is not a free man. He cannot come to us at will but must wait until others decide when to set him free.

I don't remember the circumstances of his leaving any more than how he got to us, but before school vacation ends, he's gone, and Grampa reappears. Tommy, it's decided, will stay and return to Morse High School, where, with Mumma keeping track, he'll bring his grades up to passing. Clement will go back to Uncle George and Aunt Celia. This time all his possessions go with him — the rest of his clothes, the contents of his treasure drawer — because, before you know it, the greenhouse will be sold and we will all move to Houlton.

6

Spring, 1953

Selling the greenhouse is taking longer than we expected, and, believe it or not, we're negotiating to sell it back to the very family we bought it from. There's the question of insurance. From overheard conversations, I learn that Daddy had let his lapse, and now Uncle Paul is trying to convince the insurer that Daddy couldn't be held accountable, the missed payments due to his not being in his right mind. I sit at Daddy's desk and write on his stationery, which by now I feel as entitled to as I do to my collection of junk mail.

But I have school to take up my time and also an after school activity: I have become a Brownie. Judy and Sandra also belong to the troop. We are the Chickadees, named for the official state bird of Maine. Our project is to make sit-upons. I place a whole folded section of newspaper between two squares of calico oilcloth and with black yarn sew a cross-over stitch all around the edges. This is not the kind of activity I excel at (and never want to undertake with Mumma, who knows all about sewing). Yet, in company with the other Chickadees and with someone else's mother in charge I'm happy to spend many afternoons pushing a needle through the holes punched in the oilcloth.

One day as winter is coming to an end, two cars crash into each other on Route One almost in front of the greenhouse. For hours, Charlie and I sit on our hillside by the sand pile watching. Police and ambulances screech to the scene. The road is closed off and paramedics load a woman onto a stretcher, her dark hair spilling out over a bloodied white sheet. I wonder if she will die — if she's not already dead — or if she'll be taken to a hospital and get fixed up and be sent home again the way we're waiting for

Daddy to get well and be sent home. Blood remains on the road the rest of our time in Woolwich.

On April Fool's Day I try all morning and afternoon to get up my nerve to jump from my seat in school, point to the window and yell, "Look, it's snowing!" Unlike with Mrs. Hopkins and Mrs. Scott, I hardly know where I stand with my fourth-grade teacher. Such a grandstand performance might delight her; on the other hand, it might get me sent to the hall for the rest of the year. Also, I have to ask myself: is this proper behavior for a girl? For a nine-going-on-ten-year-old girl? In this room full of quiet penciling where my written work is so awkwardly done and my reading ability apparently counts for nothing, I hardly know who I am or what I'm capable of. I don't jump up and yell.

One Saturday morning I take out the full-sized bicycle Tommy has left behind. A sleek commercial red when he got it in Patten, he's repainted it with hardware store lacquer, which in the can looked close to the original but dried is a bright cherry red seen on no other bike in the world. At the head of the driveway, I seat myself and zigzag downhill until the unguarded chain grabs my pant leg and I lose my balance and fall onto the gravel, the bike on top of me. A high school friend of Tommy's, who's been hired to work in the greenhouse, hears my cries and comes strolling out. He sets me and the bike upright again. I push the bike back to the top of the driveway, get on again, fall off again, and have again the agreeable experience of being rescued by the high school boy. I do this over and over until at last I am able to navigate from the house to the greenhouse without mishap. This day I have become a bicycle rider.

I find mice and voles by the sand pile, and one day catch a little mouse in a matchbox and ask Mumma if I can keep it. Mumma, who has a horror of rodents and can never understand the appeal of Mickey Mouse or stuffed animal mice or mice as decorations on notepaper, has a certain feeling for fellow creatures as long as they don't invade her domicile. One day when our family was new to the greenhouse, when Daddy was with us, all six of us stood on the top step of the orlight and watched one of the greenhouse cats give birth to one, two, three, four kittens. As the mother cat licked each newly emerged kitten clean I kept hoping it would shape up to be a monkey, knowing full well at seven that such a species cross-over was unlikely. Mumma and Daddy were glad to have the mother cat's natural history lesson on display for us kids. They didn't want us to be ignorant of where babies came from as some in their generation had been — probably Mumma, for instance. "Does everyone know where babies come from?" Daddy would ask from time to time, looking around the supper table, and we would assure him that we knew babies came from their mothers' bellies. (How babies got there was a bridge too far for my parents. On that question, we were left to our own resources.)

We don't name the kittens, just as we haven't named the two mother cats, which, intriguingly, are actually mother and daughter. These are work animals and feral. They keep the mice in the fields and woods where they belong and out of the house and greenhouse. This litter we watch being born — and subsequent litters — are superfluous, and so periodically, in the time-honored rural method of keeping down the adult cat population, my father kneels by the side of the greenhouse with a bucket of water and drowns kittens one by one. He doesn't like doing this; it's as distasteful as getting a plugged oil line to run free by sucking on the pipe, another task I've seen him undertake, but two cats are sufficient for keeping us free of mice, and we're not running a feline resort.

Once, one of the cats ended up in the house while we were out. We returned to find it had relieved itself on the floor and covered its deposit by leaping to a windowsill and knocking a potted plant to the floor, smashing the pot. "She was doing the best she could," Mumma said as she cleaned up the mess.

"It's a field mouse," Mumma says now, looking at the creature I've closed up in a matchbox, as though a "field mouse" were no relation to a "house mouse" and so could come under consideration as a pet. But, no, Mumma says, I can't keep it because we are really and truly moving and very soon.

Not before the Chickadees attend a big Brownie meeting in Bath, however. Up to now I have not minded wearing my school clothes to meetings even though Sandra and Judy and some of the other girls have uniforms. I'm sure that by the time of the big meeting all the other Chickadees will be in uniform, the way our leaders are urging, and after every meeting I come home and beg Mumma to buy me one. She says no in that way she has when she's made up her mind and there's no convincing her otherwise. I plead and cry, all the time knowing that I'm being unreasonable and that there's no money for anything as unnecessary as a Brownie uniform, but I can't seem to help myself. A desire to be like the other girls, to fit in, or at least not to stand out for the wrong reason, has taken possession of me.

Something similar happened in the spring of second grade when I made First Communion. All us little girls were expected to wear plain white, but Mumma asked Sister Isidore if it would be all right for me to wear the Easter dress she'd made for me that was white with a scattering of blue flowers. Mumma assured me that it was all right because Sister Isidore said it was. As we First Communicants proceeded down the aisle, I felt conspicuous to be dressed more like a flower girl than like all the miniature brides. At the same time, I was proud to be in solidarity with Sister Isidore and Mumma and in line with the constraints of our family finances. Perhaps it's with this brave concession in mind that I feel a Brownie uniform is owed me, no matter our circumstances.

Grampa drives Mumma and me into Bath to the Brownie convention, where there are apparently plenty of little girls whose circumstances are as straitened as our own because a sizable proportion are not wearing uniforms and I fit in as well as anyone else.

Another desire seizes me. I want to see friends on the weekend, aside from school and Chickadee meetings. I beg Mumma to let me ride Tommy's cherry red bike down Route One, up the road past Central School and further on to my friend Judy's house; I'm rather hazy about just where, somewhere in the area of the Chickadee meetings. Sensibly, Mumma says no, and I cry and plead in a most undignified way, secretly fearing she'll suddenly grant my plea and I'll actually have to carry out this quest. If Clement were with me, I could do it, I know. He has a knack for finding his way around — although there's only one bike; so that's a problem. If Clement were home, we might just walk to Judy's. Once when we lived in Patten he and I walked from our street down Mill Pond Road to a road that led to the outskirts of town where he happened to know that my first grade teacher lived in a farmhouse at the top of a long, steep stretch. Miss Hanson opened the door, surprised to see us but charmed I could see by Clement — blue eyes, bright complexion, dimpled chin, self-confident grin — who'd been her pupil the year before. She invited us in and served us lemonade and cookies.

I miss Clement terribly.

And then at about the one-year mark of the day they took Daddy away, negotiations over selling the greenhouse fall into place, and we are free to leave, free to go back to Houlton, our true hometown, where we will live together again as a family — except with Grampa instead of Daddy.

The final day Charlie and I ride the school bus home, we are taunted about our last name. Not comprehending a certain gesture's meaning but understanding it to be the ultimate insult, I turn before debarking and raise my middle finger, and with the other children's gasps resounding in my ears, jump to the ground and run up the driveway to the kitchen where Mumma awaits us.

7

Houlton - *Cead Mile Failte*

We arrive in Houlton on an unusually mild day in April and move into Six River Street, the first house past where the Highland Avenue Bridge crosses the Meduxnekeag River. Across the street and up a steep hill is the trim bungalow where Uncle George and Aunt Celia live. Aunt Celia's father, an immigrant from New Brunswick, Canada (and a member of the anti-Catholic KKK, Daddy later tells us), was a mail carrier, who by dint of frugal living and canny dealing managed to buy a number of properties, including the two on River Street. Aunt Celia, his beneficiary, has turned out the former tenants of Six River, the house she grew up in, so that we can move in, rent free. Although close to downtown, the rambling yellow wood-framed house and barn look as though they would be right at home on a farm. Our first evening there Aunt Celia and Mumma carry porch chairs onto the lawn and sit and talk while we kids run around. Aunt Celia has more style than Mumma and more opportunity to keep up her appearance. Although plagued from puberty by what I will later understand to be gynecological problems, she makes a fit appearance. Tall and athletic looking, she wears her hair in an upsweep that flatters her rather angular face. She has come this evening, she will confide to me years later, with a mission. A one-time elementary school teacher, she's now a full-time housewife who dotes on Meatball, the stray dog she and George took in and fattened up, and on Clement, the son they never had and don't want to give up. She's waiting for an opportune moment to ask Mumma if he could continue living with them.

We kids explore the new house, which lies perpendicular to the street, its front and back entrances facing the driveway. We enter by the glassed-in front porch, where my sit-upon has been placed on one of the rockers and will remain for the next thirty years. We open the front door and take one step up to the living room. Set in the floor under the arch that opens to the dining room is a four-foot-square register, its forced air the house's sole source of heat. We turn left in the dining room, walk to the end and enter the kitchen. Off the kitchen is the house's one bathroom — one step down because the space for it has been stolen from the back porch, the house itself dating back to the time of outhouses. At the kitchen's far end are two doors, one leading to the back porch, the other to the shed that connects the house to the barn.

At the top of the front stairs are a small front bedroom with a larger bedroom behind it and, when we walk through the larger bedroom and take a step down, a long narrow bedroom with dormers and a slanted ceiling. The door at the end of that room opens to the upper landing of the shed where rough wooden stairs lead to the lower shed. Charlie and I stride in circles around and around the entire house and shed, upstairs and down. Grampa will take the small front bedroom at the top of the stairs. Mumma will sleep in her marriage bed in the middle bedroom with me in a cot by the window. In the narrow room — almost out of range of the register — my two older brothers will share a double bed and Charlie will occupy a cot. Tommy is at work stringing his matchbook collection across the ceiling, hanging his beanies from the mirror and piling his comic books into the bins under the window seat. Clement hustles back and forth between the two houses, transferring his clothes and the contents of the treasure drawer from his private bedroom at Uncle George and Aunt Celia's to the one he'll share with his brothers. Observing his actions, Celia never makes her request.

Monday morning Charlie and I walk with Clement the short distance to St. Mary's School. At Central School in Woolwich, girls wore pants, the same as boys. Here in Houlton, Mumma seems to know that girls wear skirts and get themselves fixed up more. The night before, she did one better than metal curlers by putting my hair up in bobby pins. Unfortunately, she knew how to turn the curls in one direction only with the result that when the pins are taken out in the morning my hair sweeps by one ear and shoots out past the other. On my head, she places a straw hat with a ribbon that hangs down the back. I look more like a character out of the writings of Louisa May Alcott than a girl of the 1950s, both my mother and me a generation or two behind the times. No matter how amused my new classmates might be by the quaint appearance of this new girl whom Sister Bernard presents to her combined third and fourth grade classes, having me stand at the front of the room, they forgive me my strangeness and go out of their way to be nice to me.

At recess, my first-floor class is let out into the wide front hall of the school, built originally to be a post office. Two big girls stand behind a massive wooden table selling penny-candy: root beer barrels, squirrel nut bars, licorice twists and tootsie rolls. When the fifth and sixth graders march down the stairs from the second floor, Clement seeks me out and gives me a quarter — coming, I suppose from the allowance he gets from Aunt Celia and Uncle George — and says, "Spend five cents each day, and it will last you all week."

Then I go with my new classmates out into the gravel schoolyard, where Ann, whom Clement has picked out to be my best friend, and all the other fourth grade girls include me in their games. Unlike at Central School, we are divided according to gender, the boys playing basketball in one section that the girls are not allowed into, the girls playing jump rope or swinging on the swings in the main yard.

At noon, Clement, Charlie and I walk home to eat the lunch Mumma has prepared for us. Seeing Mumma in the middle of a school day is one of the joys of living in Houlton. Another is not having to ride a bus. Still another is the resources our town and our neighborhood offer us kids.

My first Saturday in Houlton I walk to Cary Library on Main Street, where, as a bona fide resident of the town, I qualify for a card. I select several books from the children's section, carry them home, read them and bring them back to exchange for more. "It's against the rules to take out books twice in one day," the librarian says. I am dashed. "But since this is your first day," she adds with a kindly smile, "I'll make an exception."

The houses on River Street vary from the rundown to the polished, and our neighbors are likewise mixed in fortunes and circumstances. Freddie, who lives with his grandparents farther up the street on the opposite side, is between Charlie and me in age and plays with us both. During the long spring evenings, kids play hide and seek before it's completely dark. We run through yards and under the Highland Avenue Bridge, which really old people sometimes refer to by its predecessor's name as "The Footbridge." Our games are the most fun if Wynn Lee, who's made a friend of Freddie, joins in. Wynn Lee, only a year or two out of high school, is living with her parents next door to Uncle George and Aunt Celia until her husband returns from the Korean War. I'm at first mystified when Mumma says of her, "That poor girl!" Then it strikes me that Wynn Lee is biding her time the way our family's biding our time until Daddy comes home.

On the fringe of lawn at the back side of the house, Tommy pounds a post into the ground. He screws two boards perpendicular to each other onto the post and attaches a small cross piece towards each of the four ends. He calls his construction a whirligig. Two or four children sit on the ends of the boards grasping the cross pieces. Another child grabs hold of the side of a board and runs at top speed in a circle, then ducks and crawls away, keeping her head low enough not to get whacked. The seated children get a thrilling ride, safe, too, unless the long screw Tommy used — what had come to hand when he couldn't find a bolt — twists free, causing the boards to fly into the air and crash.

Just beyond our barn, the lawn drops steeply to a flat garden only slightly elevated from the river. Each spring, we will see the Meduxnekeag churn up past its banks, over the garden and under the barn, as we hold our breath waiting to see whether it will invade the house. It never does. The Meduxnekeag, like most big Maine rivers before our own Senator Muskie champions The Clean Air Act of 1971, is a commercial dumping ground. Aunt Celia tells us that when she was a child she used to wade in it in summer and skate on it in winter. These days there's too much potato starch, white and boxy as the Styrofoam used in floral arrangements, and other pollutants for it to freeze over or for fish, other than eels, to inhabit it. Once upon a time, we're told, there was good fishing in the Meduxnekeag. Now, the only fisherman we see is an old guy who burns rubber tires under the bridge to attract the eels, which, he tells us kids, are a delicacy. We peer into his buckets at what look like sleek black snakes, and we wonder if he knows what he's talking about.

The river is pretty, nonetheless, its annual flood as beneficial to our garden as the Nile to Egypt's littoral. Just beyond our property the water enters the strip of woods that runs the length of River Street, a playground for us kids.

The spring we move in, a wrecker is demolishing the old wooden armory between our house and the approach to the Highland Avenue Bridge. Soon, bulldozers fill the foundation with earth and level an area flat as a parking lot — which it informally becomes — with steep sides descending to the pathway under the bridge, where the old guy burns tires.

That spring, or maybe the one following, Grampa gets permission to tap someone's maple trees. At Fogg's Hardware he buys galvanized buckets and appliances with borers at one end and spigots at the other. Daily, he empties the buckets, filling many gallon jugs. When one of us kids dips a finger into a bucket, the sap tastes like lightly flavored water. Mumma, doubtful about the project from the beginning, is downright alarmed when Grampa sets up a pot on the stove to boil off excess water. Sugaring, she reminds him, is supposed to take place outdoors over an open fire. Grampa knows that too, but he keeps right on, and Mumma says no more; children, even adult children, don't correct their elders. The amount of syrup yielded by all those gallons of sap is only about enough for several hearty family breakfasts of pancakes. For the next few years, until we get around to painting the kitchen, the ceiling is rimed with the fuzzy brown sugar that evaporated off the pots of sap.

Grampa prepares the garden for planting and buys a flock of chickens to house in the former harness room of the barn. Mumma approves of gardens, is mortified by the chickens. Her discomfort is soon allayed because it turns out that, since the time Grampa last lived in Houlton, the town has passed an ordinance against raising barnyard animals within town limits, and he has to return the chicks to whence they came.

The room the chickens briefly inhabited becomes a playroom for us kids. Next to it is the sleigh that Aunt Celia's father, Davey Watson, had used to deliver mail for the United States Post Office. Clement and Charlie and I take turns climbing in and out of it to take the reins. The ride is made more exciting when one of us sits inside and the other two rock the vehicle on its springs with all our might. This rowdy play lasts until Aunt Celia catches wind of it and, fearing we'll shake the ancient sleigh to pieces, forbids us to play with it anymore.

Upstairs in the barn is the hay loft, no longer storage for horse fodder but for an assortment of articles belonging to anyone who ever lived in the house back to the time when Aunt Celia herself was growing up there. At the far end of the loft is a door which swings open for the farmer to pitch hay to the horses below. Standing at the open door, Clement bends his knees, lifts his arms, yells "Geronimo!" and jumps to the driveway, landing in a crouch, then springing to his full height, his arms pumping. He dares me to do the same. "Bend your knees, land on your toes," he coaches. I hit the gravel with a jolt that runs up my legs through my torso to the very top of my head. Over the next few days, we jump over and over, never getting over the heart-in-mouth fear at the open door, the thrill of free fall, the triumph of landing on our feet.

Then Uncle George crosses the street and comes down our driveway expressly to tell us we mustn't jump from the haymow anymore. "You'll get flat feet," he says. The door is shut, perhaps nailed shut. Tommy comes into possession of a basketball hoop which he nails to the outside of the door, and that end of the driveway becomes a basketball court.

Basketball is the prime occupation of Houlton boys. At St. Mary's School, the section of the playground reserved for the boys has a hoop at each end, and there the boys pound out their pent-up energies twice during the school day and for many hours afterwards. Tommy, who belongs to an intramural team at the Rec Center — to his chagrin, he's not good enough for the high school team — has installed the hoop for his own practice, but it's Clement who puts in the most time there, and desirous of a companion to play against and coach, he enlists me. Dribbling, feinting, passing, layups, set shots and hooks — he's preparing me for a future that doesn't exist for Houlton girls. But I don't care. For me, what's important is spending the time with my brother, a brother who was taken from me and has been returned.

As summer nears, Uncle Paul gives Clement and me a job delivering advertisements for his gas and appliance store, two cents a flier. I seem to remember that we biked, but this was before we bought bikes for ourselves. We go door to door all over Houlton, and I begin to understand the layout of the town beyond the neighborhoods of River Street, Watson Avenue and Pleasant Street, where my McGillicuddy grandparents live. A town of eight thousand and the county seat, the Shiretown, Houlton is the center for the more than twenty thousand in the surrounding farm communities. And our family lives only a short walk from the epicenter: Market Square.

Old photos show a Market Square of wooden buildings. "They all burned to the ground long ago in The Great Fire," Mumma says. "Fire spreads quickly when buildings are wood. That's why the Square was rebuilt all in brick." There are still plenty of wooden buildings in town, and over the next few years a number of them go up in flames. The Congregational Church will burn to the ground one Saturday night in January — churches catch fire on Saturday nights, Mumma says, because furnaces get overheated in preparation for Sunday services. When a crowd gathers the next morning to watch the firemen douse the smoldering ruin, we see the water from the hose freeze in the air and hear it shatter when it hits the pavement.

It's possible to walk or bike all over Houlton's six square miles without ever having to cross a major highway. Also, with the exception of our street and a few others, Houlton is rich with sidewalks. All over town we kids spot Uncle Paul's delivery trucks with "Paul A. McGillicuddy" emblazoned on each side. Outside Uncle George's office overlooking Market Square a prominent sign reads, "T.H. McGillicuddy, Coal and Coke." Our name is so well known and so taken for granted it's never remarked upon. (I'm not teased about my last name again until I'm a freshman at Colby College when a sophomore coed makes a remark that causes my gorge to rise, my face to redden. All over again I am a nine year old on a school bus tormented to the point of slamming someone in the face with a lunch box or giving the entire bus the finger. In another instant, I recognize good-natured teasing for what it is and laugh, narrowly averting a socially fatal clash with my future sorority sister.)

Downtown, my classmates and I give wide berth to Helen Dobbins, an oddly-dressed, middle-aged woman with a long stride who prowls the streets loudly clearing her throat and muttering to herself. When I am with Mumma, Helen Dobbins stops to make conversation that starts out perfectly rational. She and Mumma talk about Caribou and its environs where Mumma grew up and where Helen Dobbins, as a young woman, taught school. "Your father strung up the telephone wires, there, Mary."

"Well," Mumma says. "He was the manager of the telephone office."

"He crossed the wires, Mary." Helen Dobbins raises her voice and her face contorts. "He crossed the wires in my schoolhouse."

By now I've caught on that Helen Dobbins, through no fault of my beloved Grampa Vose, suffers from crossed wires in her head. My mother makes a soothing reply, says "Nice to see you, Helen," and moves along, a guiding hand on my shoulder.

Helen Dobbins stands watching us, clearing her throat loudly enough to be heard from one end of the Square to the other. "He crossed my wires! The wires in my schoolhouse. That wasn't right, Mary. He shouldn't have done that."

At home, listening to Mumma talk with Aunt Celia and Uncle George about Helen Dobbins, I put together the story of a once bright young teacher who, when her mind gave way, returned home to live with her parents. "Streak Dobbins," Uncle George says. "We called her that because she could run like anything on the basketball court."

Streak Dobbins, I find out, is Daddy's second cousin.

"Who's your father?" This is what adults say when they hear my last name.

"Joe," I say to Mrs. French, the large, loud, rouged widow who owns and operates French's Drug Store on the corner of Main Street and Market Square.

"You look just like your father!" She pronounces this judgment loudly each time she sees me, pleasing me immensely because I'm flattered to be told I resemble my good-looking Daddy and also because I like hearing him mentioned, and that she and so many others know who he is and can place me because of him. Houlton is where he and the rest of us belong, the hometown where all of us were born and where we've resettled for good. When I'm behind the stained glass windows in French's Drug Store I imagine that back behind the counters somewhere is the door-less freight elevator that sliced off the end of one of Daddy's big toes when he worked there in high school. When I view the candies behind glass I think of the story he used to tell about the late Mr. French saying Daddy could eat all the chocolates he wanted. Daddy ate so many the first day, he felt sick. Each day after that, he ate fewer and fewer until finally he wasn't tempted to eat any ever again. Full access resulting in satiation is the obvious moral, but I know it's a flawed one because Daddy still loves chocolate. Being in French's Drug Store makes me feel close to Daddy, especially when Mrs. French peers at me from over the counter and exclaims, "You look just like your father!"

After 10:30 Mass at St. Mary's, clusters of kin linger outside the white, steepled, New England style church which looks all the world like its Protestant counterparts. While visitors to Houlton or residents of less than a good chunk of their lifetime — "people from away" — walk silently to their cars, we greet our McGillicuddy relatives — "vestibuling," as Daddy used to call it. Uncle George is here, while Aunt Celia, contrary to the norm, attends services at the Court Street Baptist Church. Theirs is a "mixed marriage," not sinful like an "attempted marriage" — that is, one involving a Catholic marrying outside the Church — but less than ideal.

Uncle Paul is here along with Aunt Pauline, who took the more conventional route of converting to Catholicism when she got married. An interesting fact about Aunt Pauline is that she's part Indian. What part and just who this Indian was no one can tell us, but once we kids know this about her, we can't help but see the Indian in her: her straight black hair pulled back into a chignon, her dark eyes and dark skin (compared to ours) that tans deeply each summer, her quiet dignity, which Indians have a reputation for.

Aunt Dorothy and Uncle Bert, who recently moved away, may have returned for the weekend, drawn back to a St. Mary's more familiar than the one in Bangor. Aunt Mary may be back, too, although she's acclimated to Bangor perhaps better than Aunt Dorothy ever does. One fine summer Sunday finds Uncle Ned and Aunt Nora present, up from South Boston for an annual visit. We cousins add more than a dozen members to the family mix although, to my disappointment, there isn't among them another girl my age. Grampa and Mumma know many other congregants as well, people we aren't related to but some of whom have known Grampa since he was manager of the telephone office and Mumma since she was Mary Vose — "Miss Vose," if she taught them at Houlton High School.

In Houlton, our relatives' doors are open to us and we enter without knocking, just as Clement foretold, and are welcomed with smiles. Uncle George and Aunt Celia we visit almost daily. They kiss each other in front of us whenever Uncle George leaves the house or arrives home. If we all leave the house together and they get into their car to go on an errand, Uncle George opens the passenger side door for Aunt Celia before going around to the driver's side. (Daddy will say, in a disapproving sort of a way, that they behave this way, doting on each other, because they never had children.) Their kitchen cabinets smell of spices and chocolate and citron. Unlike Mumma's cookies, rather dry oatmeal and raisin, Aunt Celia's are sugary, gooey confections with chocolate chips in place of raisins. Aunt Celia has a bag of small rubber interlocking blocks she keeps for visiting children, and because of their novelty we continue to play with them long after we've outgrown such things. I sit on the hassock in her living room, happy to find one more adult willing to listen to me go on and on. "Barbara," she says very pleasantly after a while. "Can't you stop moving?" Then I continue talking but stop pummeling and rocking the hassock until I get so carried away with my story that I start moving again, and she doesn't say anything more about it.

After Uncle George and Aunt Celia's, the home we visit most often is that of Grampa and Nana McGillicuddy. We enter the white wood-framed house through a woodshed into a pink and grey kitchen presided over until recently by three handsome, grey-haired, pink-cheeked old people: Nana and Grampa and Aunt Kit. Aunt Kit is Grampa's sister. Never married, she clerked for many years in the ladies department of Rhines, a fine department store in Bangor. Even as her mind began to fail, she dressed with an eye to fashion, applied subtle make-up to her face and a tint of bluing to her short, stylish curls. Not known for having a knack for handling kids, she nevertheless paid us mind by giving each of her many grandnieces and grandnephews an expertly wrapped Christmas gift signed, "From Aunt Kit and Santa," and long after I saw this as a sort of joke I continued to think of her as having a special relationship with the jolly old St. Nick pictured in Coke ads. She was still living with Grampa and Nana in the fall when Tommy was there and he laughs about her habit, in spite of eating the meals Nana prepared, of keeping a supply of peanut butter, saltines and a few other items separate from the rest of the household and about how vigilant she was that he not help himself to them. Once, when I was about six and my family was making a day visit from Patten, Daddy and I drove over from Watson Avenue to Pleasant Street. I felt sick to my stomach and stayed in the car while he went in to say hi. After a while he came out to check on me and found that I'd opened the car door and vomited onto the driveway. Shoving gravel over the mess with his foot, Daddy praised me for having the presence of mind not to throw up all over the car — which, he assured me, any one of my three brothers would have done. Then I lay down on the back seat and he went back into the house. A few minutes later, Aunt Kit appeared at the car door with a glass of water and two or three of her very own saltines.

When her forgetfulness worsened she was moved farther up Pleasant Street to Uncle Paul and Aunt Pauline's home, where there were more and younger people to keep an eye out for her. She distressed Aunt Pauline by never accepting dark-haired, teenaged Terry as part of the household. "Who's that Indian?" she'd ask. "How did he get in here?" It wasn't until the day she slipped out of the house in her nightgown and had to be pursued halfway down Pleasant Street that the family decided to place her in a nursing home.

As young adults, Aunt Kit and Grampa and their siblings crossed the border from New Brunswick to Maine to seek employment. A Saturday night fiddler, Grampa got to attend dances and get paid as well. Perhaps it was at a dance that he met my grandmother. She grew up in Houlton on the farm her father was awarded after serving in the Civil War. (The story is that he got the farm because he'd lost a limb, but whether it was an arm or a leg is a detail the story doesn't supply.) After graduating from high school, she finished a year of teacher training — as did her sisters — and at the time she met Grampa was teaching in a one-room school. When her new husband wanted to have letterhead printed up as "Tom Mack," she insisted he spell out his whole name. Although he included colorful cuss words in his speech, he had to curb himself at home, and she did not allow such talk from her children. Her grown children's colorful language, for the most part, remained respectable. "Holy limpin' lightnin' Ponto," my grown father might say or "Gee willikers!" Exasperated, Daddy might refer to a thing or a person as "cuss-ed."

Despite her insistence on good manners, Nana was a gentle soul. It was Grampa who ruled the family — the story was that he grew up ordering his own parents around — and who made himself hard to please. I am aware, even as a child, that Daddy resented having to work as hard as he did as a boy and having to redo tasks that didn't measure up to Grampa's high standards. "My father was the world's first efficiency expert," Daddy will later say, with grudging admiration.

And, yet, there were limits in that time and place for autocratically-minded heads of families. His equally strong-minded sisters, for instance, sometimes gave him "what-for." Kit, for instance, told him he mustn't wear red neckties because they clashed with his red face, and Margaret apparently gave him what-for about Nana's last pregnancy, a rather late-in-life occurrence. Both sisters — and maybe Nana's sisters as well — quickly shamed him out of an idea he floated about keeping Ned, his oldest, out of high school to help on the farm.

By the time I know them, all my grandparents have false teeth, although Grampa McGillicuddy until a late, devastating onset of receding gum disease hadn't had a cavity his whole life. Now he suffers from rheumatism and walks on bent legs with a cane. He smells of the peppermints he eats to calm his troublesome stomach.

In actual fact, every child is the product of a mixed marriage, and no matter how much the bride and groom's families may appear to outsiders to resemble each other, a grandchild senses striking differences. On the rare occasions when my two grandfathers are together, they are polite. Peers, they call each other Tom and Arthur, not the "Mister" that my parents employ for their fathers-in-law. Grampa Vose does the most talking, recounting, as is his conversational style, his accomplishments of the day — got up at 5:30, for instance, picked berries before breakfast and so on in a bed-to-bed account reminiscent of an issue of the "Spuds Special" that Tommy finds pretty corny.

Grampa McGillicuddy smiles genially, nods approvingly, but I think maybe he's laughing at Grampa Vose (although, to be fair, no more than he laughs at everyone) and that afterwards he may repeat my other grandfather's recitation to get a laugh from other McGillicuddys, namely his sons and daughters, who behind their backs refer to Mumma's parents as "Ma and Pa Vose."

Pa Vose, I see through McGillicuddy eyes, lacks a nimble wit and, although a good man, is perhaps a bit stuck on himself and therefore a bit of a bore. And maybe behind Grampa McGillicuddy's jokey attitude lurks something like class resentment. By the time Irish Catholics arrived in New Brunswick all the best land was already being farmed by the Protestant Scotch Irish. In Maine, too, the best land and the thriving businesses were owned by the descendants of the early, Protestant settlers. Grampa worked hard all his life, running a hardscrabble farm, laboring in the woods, buying and selling first lumber and then coal and its softer cousin coke, in a never-ending effort to as Dad would say "get ahead," which resulted in his barely keeping his head above water and perhaps made Arthur Vose's comparatively easy success hard to take. As is the case generally with top dogs, Grampa Vose never seems to pick up on any underdog attitude in Grampa McGillicuddy.

Unlike Grampa Vose, who doesn't "make remarks" about people and whose jokes and sense of humor are generally good-natured and corny, Grampa McGillicuddy is witty — especially at the expense of other people. He has nicknames for everyone. The old couple, for instance, who walk all over town all day long he refers to as Thunder and Lightning because you never see one without the other. Retired from T. H. McGillicuddy Coal and Coke, Grampa drives downtown most days and parks in Market

Square to watch the people go by. If we kids happen along, he toots his horn and we get into his car that smells of peppermint and visit for a while. "She's suing the town, you know," he says about a short old woman who walks by. He looks at us judiciously.

"Why?" we kids ask.

"For building the sidewalks too close to her backside, hee, hee, hee." For an old man, Grampa has a boyish laugh.

Nana McGillicuddy is never in the car with Grampa in Market Square. In fact she's never in the car with him anywhere because she doesn't leave her house. Not to shop or attend Mass or call on a relative or friend. As a child, I just accept Nana's stay-at-home state. When as a young adult, I say to Mumma, "Isn't it odd that Nana never went out?" she agrees. A homebody and with a marked preference for her children to play only with their cousins or closest neighbors, Nana, Mumma tells me, was always inclined to keep to herself. Then, once years ago, she was dressed up and in the car ready to ride to Boston to have a hysterectomy, when at the last minute she lost her nerve, went back into the house and never came out again.

Perhaps Nana's happiest days were when her young adult children were mostly grown and mostly still living at home. When setting the supper table, she counted in and then subtracted Ned, who was working in South Boston, living with an uncle and aunt and attending pharmacy school at night. Joe, my father, was town treasurer and attended Houlton Business School at night. George, before and after the one semester he was able to scrounge up the money to attend the University of Maine, chauffeured well-to-do people. Dorothy clerked at the Five and Dime and became engaged to the manager, a sophisticate from Boston. Paul was in high school — no great shakes as a scholar but president of his class all four years — and raising chickens to sell. "Paul could always turn a nickel into a dime," Nana said of him. Pre-teen Mary prayed every night for a bicycle. (Years later, when she jokingly confided this to her brothers, they felt awful. When they were kids, the family couldn't afford bikes, but if only she had voiced her prayers aloud, they'd have gladly pitched in to see that she had one.) As a teenager she had the leisure to be on the high school tennis team, a sport she played most of the rest of her life; being the youngest did confer certain advantages.

In those days Nana and Grampa's house was a gathering place for their children and their children's friends, cousins, and sweethearts (my mother and father alternating Sunday dinner at Daddy's with Mrs. Donald's boarding house), and Nana enjoyed engaging the young people in conversation. "Say a big word," she said one day to one of my father's business school friends.

"Circumstances-alter-cases," the young rube replied, inadvertently becoming a character in the store of family stories.

When Tommy was a baby, Mumma tells me, she took him out every morning in his carriage to buy the day's groceries and every day she called on Nana McGillicuddy. One day Nana told Mumma about Lawrence, the toddler between Ned and my father in age, who died in her arms of pneumonia. "The doctor had come," Mumma quotes Nana saying. In other words, in those days before antibiotics, everything that could be done was done. When Mumma repeated Nana's story to Daddy, it was the first time he'd ever heard tell of Baby Lawrence. Nana is fond of babies, Mumma says, and enjoys them most as newborns when they lie peacefully in one's arms, before they make a stir of themselves.

After all her children left for homes of their own, even Mary going off to secretarial jobs first in Island Falls and then in Bangor, Nana became despondent. I know from Tommy that sometimes she would be so morose at supper that Grampa in exasperation would flick the last speck of water from his glass at her from across the table. (Flicking water across the table at an unwary child was such a common amusement for my grandfather that Daddy carried it over into his dealings with us kids.)

When I'm grown up, I will discover that Nana's mother was also subject to depression and that a few years before my father was born, when she was widowed and living at the family farm with several of her adult children, she escaped their vigilance long enough to hang herself in the barn. (Apparently, mental sickness

74

coursed through both sides of Dad's family. "Melancholy ran in the Denning line," he said once, referring to his paternal grandmother's family name.)

These days Nana doesn't appear sad. She sits in the kitchen rocker in a housedress, her long grey braids twisted around her head. She, too, is witty but not at other people's expense. Every day she enjoys a long telephone visit with her cousin Mame Dobbins — mother of Streak — who gets out and about, gathering news to share. Although Nana doesn't mingle, she likes to hear about other people or to spy them walking past her kitchen windows. And she greets us kids warmly, calling Charlie "Charlsie." With Grampa, I'm often a little uneasy, uncertain of whether I pass muster, but with Nana, as with Grampa Vose, I feel cherished. Indeed, everyone who comes into her kitchen — my uncles and aunts and cousins, even Fred, Grampa's hired man, loves Nana.

Like Mumma and Grampa Vose and Aunt Celia, Nana listens to me talk. She asks the names of my schoolmates and tells me what she knows of their families and whether they're related to me. From Nana, I learn that in addition to my first cousins, I have many second and third cousins and even, in Mary Ellen McCluskey, who is in the third grade division of Sister Bernard's classroom, someone who is both a second and third cousin.

"You and I will go visit Aunt Kit," Mumma says one day. We walk to downtown, up Court Street and off onto a side street to the Folsom Home, a large old brown building that looks as though it really was once some family's home. We mount the steps to the porch and enter a hall that smells vaguely of old people. A nurse appears and Mumma says who we're there to visit. We're shown to a parlor and soon Aunt Kit comes in. Her hair is as much blue as silver, her pink and white skin almost translucent, her blue eyes opened wide in her delight to see us. Retaining the tune if not the sense of her former occupation, she fingers the lapel of Mumma's old spring coat and says, "It's what they're all wearing this season!"

75

Every few months after that first visit, Mumma urges me to pay a visit to the Folsom Home. Aunt Kit continues to decline. One day she shows me a magazine open to the picture of a baby and tells me that she found the baby on a shelf in the basement and brought it up to her room to care for. The more she talks about the baby the more distressed she becomes over its plight. At home I report the visit to Mumma as I have all of the previous ones and I, too, am agitated. Eventually, Mumma stops reminding me to visit Aunt Kit.

(The last time I see Kit is a few years hence when I visit the home as part of a group of carolers. After our first few songs I separate myself from the others and go looking for her. I find her in a room alone, curled up in a crib, a mad smile on her face, her eyes the bright blue of her brother's, my Grampa McGillicuddy. In fact, with her hair skinned back and her skull so prominent, she could be his twin, his mad twin.)

Having relatives all over town, we settle into Houlton almost as smoothly as though we'd never lived elsewhere.

My parents, Christmas 1935

Me with Tommy and Clement in Houlton, 1946

Me in Houlton, 1946

1947

Tommy in Patten, 1949

Tommy took this picture with his new Brownie camera, 1949

Nana and Grampa Vose

Nana and Grampa McGillicuddy

Tommy in his high school yearbook

The picture of me from Dad's wallet

Charlie in Woolwich

6 River Street, Houlton, Maine

Me as a sixth grader in St. Mary's School

Clement and Charlie in Houlton, 1956

8

Summer 1953

During the summer in Houlton we kids are as free to roam as we were in Woolwich, with the added enhancements of sidewalks and playmates. The shortcuts kids take through unfenced yards to get to each other's houses and the fruits of the trees we help ourselves to belong as much to us as to anyone. Fenced yards signify mean-spirited people, and there are those among us who feel justified in creeping up to their front doors at dusk, ringing the bell and skedaddling to a tree distant enough to feel safe, close enough to witness the enraged owner shaking his fist and yelling.

We help ourselves to yellow transparents, the first apples to ripen in summer, and throw the cores into bushes with the thought that we are propagating more of these sweet treats for the next generation. "Money doesn't grow on trees," Daddy used to say, but other people's orchards do offer a feeling of abundance. Green apples look tempting, but it doesn't take more than one good bellyache to teach us to hold off until the skin blushes and the seeds turn from white to brown. Chokecherries grow next to Freddie's front door — and all over the place like the weeds that they are. I am too old to really believe what the other kids say about them, that if you eat chokecherries and drink milk at the same time, you'll die, but it's a deliciously scary idea.

By our front steps, plants with bushy yellow flowers shoot up tall. A stand of bamboo separates our drive from the driveway that goes under the bridge. Two wicker chairs in the center of the fronds where once a well house must have stood offer a cool refuge from the summer sun, a private place to play or talk.

The barn has a cupola with a window in each of its four sides. Bats — or maybe birds of some sort, maybe owls — want to nest there, and we kids think it a good idea, but Mumma is mortified. What would people think? The trespassers must be flushed out, the windows sealed.

On the back porch is a clothes line and out the back door an aluminum clothes tree, a shaft with four sides, like the cupola, with plastic lines. Suddenly more insistent on my helping her, Mumma acquaints me with the clothes basket. Underwear, for propriety's sake, I know to hang on the shorter inside lines of the tree, outerwear on the outside lines.

Although I resist working with Mumma I'm always pleased to be part of any project Tommy proposes. One day he decides to edge the lawn and assigns sections to each of us younger kids. One corner he cuts with a curved flourish that I find very artistic. Sticking out into the driveway as the flourish does, right next to where we alight from the car, it soon loses all its grass, but even as bald earth it reminds me of the thrill of being part of any enterprise of Tommy's.

Mrs. Donald appears at the top of our driveway, not having phoned ahead — no one here phones ahead. Mumma is all aflutter, running around gathering newspapers and fluffing couch pillows, as Mrs. Donald, a character from Mumma's stories, slowly descends the drive. Mumma opens the door and exclaims over our guest, who's dressed in dark old-fashioned clothing like an illustration from one of Mumma's childhood books. They sit in the living room, Mrs. Donald in the arm chair just inside the door, Mumma on the end of the couch, leaning forward, the better to hear. She's smiling. I see that she loves Mrs. Donald and basks in the older woman's complete good will.

Every once in a while after that, Mrs. Donald pays us a visit. Mumma calls her "Mrs. Donald" and so do we kids. Mrs. Donald has a husband whom everyone calls "Herbie Donald." Other drivers know to steer clear when Herbie Donald is behind the wheel of his car. Stories abound of his accidents and near accidents; yet no one presumes to take away his license. Daddy used to get a kick out of Herbie Donald, Mumma tells me, when the older man presided over the table at the boarding house, offering such bits of wisdom as, "Whiskey when you're sick makes you well; whiskey when you're well makes you sick." Herbie Donald could be cuss-ed, but you had to love him.

The Donalds had a son and a daughter, Mumma tells me. One day when the daughter was a beautiful young woman still living at home she reached to a high shelf in her closet and felt a lump under her arm. She died of breast cancer. Their handsome son Fred graduated from Bates College the year after Mumma finished Colby. When she lived at the Donalds', Fred was there, too, and worked at a bank. He was at dinner every night and Sunday noontime, so both Mumma and Daddy knew him well.

After Mumma and Daddy got married and one or another of her old Colby chums would come to visit, they'd sometimes invite Fred to be a fourth at dinner. Always charming to his dinner companion, he disappointed Mumma by never following up — inviting the guest to go for a walk the next day, for instance, or to attend a movie. When beautiful Eleanor, Mumma's Colby chum, fellow Ogunquit waitress, and Grand Tour companion, came for a visit and Fred was the fourth, Mumma warned her ahead of time not to expect anything from him. Before dessert was served, Fred had fallen in love with Eleanor. He tried to spend every bit of the rest of the weekend with her. Eleanor kept taking Mumma aside and saying, "But I don't see what's wrong with him."

"Nothing's wrong with him," Mumma would say. "We've just never seen him act like this before."

Fred and Eleanor were married within the year, and now live not far from us with their son and daughter.

As for Mrs. Donald, she will continue to drop in from time to time, looking even older and more frail year after year. (Once, when Clem and I are in high school, Mum spots Mrs. Donald, now widowed, hesitating at the top of our drive where the boys have failed to chop the ice or to scatter sand. "Quick," she instructs Clem, "Go see to it Mrs. Donald doesn't fall." Clem hurries out and offers Mrs. Donald his arm. Halfway down the path, he slips and, to his chagrin, the deceptively frail-looking old lady holds on and keeps him from landing on his backside.)

Two things Grampa Vose loves are eating and socializing. During the spring and summer of 1953, he takes the whole family to church suppers, including at the Protestant churches, where for a reasonable price we sit at long tables and eat meals based on whatever's coming into season. When we attend Saturday night potlucks at our own St. Mary's, Mumma brings baked beans. We kids have eaten Mumma's baked beans and steamed brown bread along with a vegetable — usually cabbage salad — every Saturday night for our whole lives. Everyone we know eats baked beans on Saturday night. Mumma always bakes big beans because that's what she and Daddy prefer. So at a potluck I fill up on little beans, and I think about Daddy and wonder why it is that he doesn't like little beans. Daddy doesn't like milk either. "Milk is for the calf," he used to tell us kids. "You're stealing the calf's milk." But we know he was kidding and we go right on relishing large cold glasses of milk — chocolate in Charlie's case — which Mumma never stints on even though she can't stand to drink milk either.

Everything reminds me of Daddy, and in a part of my mind, I'm always thinking about him even though it's Grampa I'm spending time with.

When Grampa takes the car out on errands I'm often in the passenger seat, entrusted with looking out for traffic approaching from the right. "You weren't paying attention to your side!" he scolds me once after a near miss. Always on the lookout for a deal, he introduces me to everyone he stops to buy from, sell to or swap with, conversation being the grease of every negotiation. "This is Mary and Joe's daughter," he says, and, although he introduces me as "Barbara," he addresses me as "Ruth" and is perplexed when others follow his example. Listening to Grampa talk to strangers about my family I understand that Daddy will never return to public office, that promoters and voters don't trust a man who's spent time in a mental hospital. "It's not fair," Grampa says to his listeners, summing up the perfidy of former supporters, and I silently agree.

That first summer in Houlton, Grampa plans a car trip for the whole family. We'll go to Aunt Ruth and Uncle Norman's outside Philadelphia. He maps out the route, figuring he and Tommy will switch driving every one hundred miles by the odometer. Afterwards Tommy laughs good-naturedly — mostly — about how strictly Grampa adheres to the one hundred mile rule, changing drivers amid city traffic or on a limited-access parkway, barely willing, if the odometer registers a new one hundred in the middle of a bridge, to wait to get to the far side.

Aunt Ruth is tall and angular, has red hair, a gap between her two front teeth and a dramatic flair. The mother of three boys, all younger than I, she exclaims over me and makes of me as though I'm the daughter she'll never have. She exclaims over Mumma as well, pronouncing how smart my mother is, how accomplished, how good-looking. Childhood stories spill from her lips, stories in which, "May-ree" — as she pronounces Mumma's name — excels, while she, the younger sister, is nowhere near as clever.

I feel the bond Aunt Ruth establishes between us. I, too, am nowhere near as smart or accomplished as Mumma. I, too, would rather leave household chores to Mumma, who does them so much more efficiently and cleverly than I. No wonder Grampa so often addresses me as Ruth. She and I are two of a kind.

And yet, she and Uncle Norman are living a much more sophisticated life than what I'm used to seeing. For one thing, they have cocktails every night before dinner. (I don't remember whether Grampa and Mumma partook while we were there, but I think perhaps they did, as they did not consider themselves teetotalers.) Uncle Norman, when he arrives home from his job at an engineering firm in the city, is the one to prepare the drinks. A few inches shorter than Aunt Ruth and several years older, he's quieter than she but equally witty and welcoming, a perfect host. Another thing about Uncle Norman is that, like Aunt Celia and like Grampa before he converted, he's a Protestant. He's not interested in converting, we are given to understand, but he doesn't object to his children being raised Catholic and that's the main thing.

During summer in Houlton I'm not cut off from other girls my age the way I was in Woolwich. For one thing, the town recreational department offers free swimming lessons. I'm issued a white, silver-rimmed cardboard disk listing my name and level and attached to a cord to hang around my neck. Three mornings a week I walk up to the Rec Center across from my grandparents' house and board a yellow school bus that drives our beginner class three or four miles out to a swim area at Nickerson Lake for our 8:30 class. Dressed only in our swimsuits in the chilly Aroostook air, we do calisthenics, the instructor, a burly college man with dark frizzy hair, forbidding us to shiver, as shivering he says would only make us feel colder. Not exactly a natural at swimming, I'm capable of learning and over the next few years I keep at the lessons right through Junior Life Saving.

I tell Nana all about my beginner lessons and she tells me that the burly, frizzy-haired instructor is a distant cousin.

I live within walking distance of other girls my age, my St. Mary's classmates. Ann, the best friend Clement picked out for me, lives in a stone and wood-framed cottage bursting with four kids, two more to be born before we graduate from grammar school. Her mother, whose Franco-American accent is more pronounced whenever she returns from a stay with her sisters who live in Massachusetts mill towns, is usually warm and welcoming, although occasionally harried and fed up, at which times we kids know to stay clear of her. Of an artistic bent, she fashions decorations and delicacies and hand-sewn garments for every holiday and special occasion, stealing time by staying up late into the night. Ann's father, like Grampa McGillicuddy, grew up on a farm in New Brunswick and immigrated to Maine as a young man trading in on his home-grown skills as a carpenter. Although vigorous and lithe, he's also balding and older than everyone else's parents — come his birthday, he's an astonishing fifty years of age.

Until the youngest, a second girl, is born, Ann has a light, airy bedroom all to herself with ample space for her dolls, her cowboy hats and guns and her Hardy Boy mysteries. Although we both love our dolls, Ann and I are tomboys.

At my house, Ann and I go into the boys' room and rummage through the comics under the window seat. We particularly like the cowboy ones: Gene Autry, the Lone Ranger, Roy Rogers and Dale Evans. Ann is fond of horses, and when we play outside we each hitch along on one leg, one hand holding the reins, the other slapping a thigh and keep up a steady set of directions to our steed — Trigger or Silver or Buttermilk. Ann puts two fingers into her mouth and emits a whistle that can be heard from the other side of the Highland Avenue Bridge.

Much of our playtime is spent outdoors, where we stalk each other through the woods playing cowboys and Indians or combine forces in the shadow of the Highland Avenue Bridge to solve crime as Frank and Joe Hardy. One afternoon we come across a patch of soft tar and spend hours working it like clay to produce an array of miniature sculptures. Mumma doesn't mind when I play hard enough to get my clothes really dirty. But when I come home that day, streaked with tar, she, who is rarely angry at me, is furious. She purses her lips and says, "There's no need of that!" — tar and burdocks, it turns out, being twin *bêtes noires*.

Tar and burdocks are never a temptation for another new friend, Mary — one of four Marys among the dozen or so girls in our class — who has a penchant for more sedate play. Mary lives near the downtown in a large white house set at the back of a spacious lawn. Except for Uncle Paul and Aunt Pauline's, it's grander than other houses with which I'm familiar. The front door on the wide front porch opens onto a central hallway, living and dining room on one side, study and kitchen on the other. At the back of the house, between kitchen and dining room is a butler's pantry — sans butler, naturally. Equally unusual is the presence of a half bath on the first floor, making a trek up the hardwood stairs to the main bathroom unnecessary for visitors, also allowing for the phenomenon of two people in the house using toilets simultaneously. A spacious bedroom takes up each of the four corners of the upstairs. Mary's is the one with the sleeping porch, an unheated room over the shed, accessed by crawling through a window in her room. Mary's two younger brothers occupy another room, and when her baby sister is born, the guest room is turned into a nursery.

Big bedroom all to herself, sleeping porch, full attic, cozy shed, neat barn-turned-garage — Mary's house is a girls' delight, and Mary, while the rest of us have to wheedle permission to have more than one friend sleep over at a time, commands enough sway in her household to regularly host slumber parties. Mary's mother is a trained nurse. Like all the mothers, she doesn't now work outside the home, but unlike the others, she doesn't appear to be particularly busy. After school, she sits in the living room, *Newsweek* magazine on her lap, smoking and talking with us girls. Mary's father, a lawyer, is involved in state and local politics. On occasion, he hosts visiting politicians and after baby Eileen is born Mary must temporarily vacate her room whenever a guest spends the night. One morning she comes to school proudly announcing that the night before Governor Muskie slept in her bed — an innocent use of a loaded phrase her schoolmates tease her about forever after.

In time for school to start, a girl a year ahead of me moves into the house next to ours. Mary Ann is from New Jersey. Her parents sound like our Woolwich neighbors the Werters, who called each other "Mr. Whiter" and "Mrs. Whiter." The Bartinoskis have come to Houlton because Mary Ann's father has taken a job at the weather station at the airport. On a sun room off the kitchen he operates a ham radio station, and that's usually where he is when he's home. Bill Boy, Mary Ann's little brother, spends his time digging a deeper and deeper hole in the foreshortened front yard. Their house is built into the hillside, the entrance on the street side opening to the first floor. Down a steep driveway, there's a door leading to the basement. At the far end of the basement beyond the furnace, the wooden floor ends and we step down into an area as large as a good-sized room, where Mary Ann and I construct a bachelorette apartment. We — meaning Mary Ann primarily with me assisting — put up cast-off drapes to divide the space into a living room and a dressing room. Somehow, we find enough old armchairs and end tables and ashtrays to make the living room cozy. In the dressing room, we hang our mothers' (and no doubt Aunt Celia's) cast-off skirts and dresses. We repair to this haven frequently to dress up, discuss our careers, smoke fake cigarettes and handle imaginary phone calls. Ongoing decorating and housekeeping also keep us busy. When the weather's nice we sometimes transport our domestic scenes to the paths and clearings in the ribbon of woods that extends along the river. In Mary Ann, I've found the perfect next door neighbor. And in her mother the perfect advocate for girlish ventures.

All the mothers are in their houses when I visit, and my mother, who's home most of the time anyway, is always home when I have anyone over. My friends' fathers come and go, greeting us, making small talk, teasing us a little. They're like my Daddy, only they're home part of every day and sleep at home every night, something my Daddy hasn't done for many months. I yearn for Daddy. A good part of my mind is fully occupied by a vision of our family reunited.

9

Fall 1954

When school starts, Charlie stays downstairs in Sister Dennis's combined first and second grade classroom, while I move upstairs to the fifth and sixth grade room. This is young Sister Gemma's first year in Houlton and she doesn't yet have her fifty-plus students straight in her veiled and wimpled head when she comments to another Sister that she thinks Clement must be sweet on Barbara. Maybe she got this impression because whenever Clement gets back a paper with a good mark, he stands up from his seat in the front of the room with the other sixth graders and walks to the back of the room between the columns of dark, wooden, bolted-to-the-floor desks to show it to me.

School is in session for less than a month when it halts for the three-week potato-picking recess, which kids refer to as "pickin' batatters" or simply "pickin". Now that we are fifth graders, almost all my classmates expect to pick. Cobina, who lives on a farm at the outskirts of town, invites my friends and me — and Clement, too — to work for her father. For this hard, dirty work, Mumma gives me a pair of dungarees Clement has outgrown. (I will pick potatoes all through grammar school and high school, always in dungarees Clem has outgrown.)

Cobina's father drives his pickup into town, and Clement and I and Ann and her brother Peter and the other children who are part of our crew sit on benches facing each other in the canopied truck bed, our lunch boxes on our knees. Because we are performing hard labor, Mumma has doubled our sandwiches and abandoned peanut butter and jelly for chicken or turkey. She's also included a piece of crunchy fruit or vegetable and — for energy — a five-cent chocolate bar. Once at the field, we are each given a rubber-banded packet of tickets, a woven Indian basket with a handle and an allotted section to work in. Mr. Hannigan drives his tractor up and down the field, dragging a digger that scoops the potatoes from underground, sifts them across a rattling bed of chains, and deposits them atop the freshly churned soil. Shuffling along on my hands and knees, I pick up potatoes and drop them into the basket. When the basket's full, I stand and heave it to one knee and stagger to a barrel to dump it. Four baskets fill a barrel; four barrels equal a dollar's pay. Between the hoop and the staves at the rim of each full barrel, I wedge one of the tickets with my number on it. At the end of the day, Cobina's mother will sort and count tickets and start a tally for each of us workers to determine what we are owed at week's end. At noon, the digger stops and we kids congregate next to the woods to eat our lunches. Our toilet is the woods, which we walk into individually to find a secluded spot — with a log to perch on if necessary. We wipe our bottoms with leaves and "wash" our hands by rubbing them in the dirt.

The hour for our lunch not up, we play cowboys and Indians in the woods. After a while we hear the tractor starting up, but we are having too much fun sneaking around in gangs and ambushing each other to go back to work. Our sections get further and further behind. When we emerge from the woods we're dismayed to see how many rows of freshly unearthed potatoes await us. Mr. Hannigan stops the tractor in order to let us catch up. At five o'clock, we stop for the day.

Each morning for the rest of the week we ride to the field to receive tickets, baskets and sections. Each day we work less and play more, our games of cowboys and Indians becoming increasingly more fierce. War whoops and "Geronimo!" and mad gallops intersperse with eerie silences. I gain a reputation for being able to disappear in the foliage and sneak up on others without cracking any sticks underfoot. At the end of each day, Clement and I return home in the back of the pickup muddy, all played out and hungry for Mumma's hearty supper. During potato picking season, we take baths every single evening. Our bathroom is

94

almost as cold as the porch because until my parents remodel after we kids have grown up, there's no radiator in there — and no shower. Ordinarily, we kids take turns bathing once a week on Saturdays, filling in with sponge baths and shampoos in the sink. But ordinarily we don't get filthy dirty the way we do picking potatoes. A tub full of hot water warms the room and soothes the body.

"This wouldn't even pay for the lunches I fix!" Mumma says when Clement and I arrive home on Friday with our meager earnings. She and Tommy decide that for the remainder of potato picking season Clement and I will travel with him up Route One where he works with his high school friend Max Miller.

We arrive before the digger has started up, and it's so cold we sit on barrels and bang our feet against the staves to get the circulation going. For most of the rest of the day, I kneel in freshly turned dirt and fill my basket. The early morning dew dampens my shins and the occasional stinky, rotten potato wets through my gloves. Rocks in the soft soil bruise my knees. (One season a few years hence, we kids keep getting boils on our knees. At White's Drug Store, Mumma buys a jar of poultice which every evening she heats on the stove and which after our baths we slather onto our knees, wrapping them with gauze.)

In this field there is no time to run in the woods playing cowboys and Indians. I must work consistently to keep up with my section, stopping only for the lunch hour. The sky can be limitless blue or blue with scudding clouds or overhung with grey. The air can be crisp, misty or hot. The weather changes from day to day and within each day. From early morning to mid-afternoon, I peel off my clothes a layer at a time and then I start adding them back. In these few short weeks, the leaves of the deciduous trees surrounding the fields turn to orange, red and yellow. Before me and behind me are Clement and the other pickers. The adult pickers are mostly Indian women. Unlike us kids who shuffle forward on our knees, they stand and bend over, scooping so quickly that many fill one hundred barrels a day, twice the number I'll ever achieve even as a junior and senior in high school.

I hear the digger approaching, drowning out the natural sounds of field and woods. Willard Miller, Max's father, looks down at me from the tractor seat. "What time is it, Willard?" I call out.

Willard stretches his neck to look up at the sun, then over the whole sky. "Eleven o'clock," he says.

Another hour till lunch.

He pulls his pocket watch out of his overalls. "Yup, eleven o'clock." Although Clement has pointed out that Willard is asked the time so frequently as he chugs down the field that he's going more by his watch than by the movement of the sun, to me he's enchantingly wise and knowledgeable about all things in the natural world. Like Daddy.

I just know Daddy would like potato picking. We could share a section, a big section that together we could reap a hundred barrels from. By the time the sun reaches its height, I have thrown off jacket, scarf and sweater. I keep on the cotton kerchief, which keeps my hair out of the way but does nothing to shield my face from the sun. To ease the burning, I pat my face with damp soil. I keep moving, potatoes to basket, basket to barrel. The rhythm of the work and of the day, the beauty of the surroundings, the feeling of being part of a shared enterprise, the freedom to daydream or let my mind wander — I am at home here in the potato field.

And yet, I'm not keeping up. First two, then four, then six rows behind. On either side of me, others are staying level with the digger, even though they all have sections longer than mine. I spot the truck that picks up the barrels making its way down the field at a crawl. Max and Tommy are on the back, operating a device that clamps onto barrels and hoists them onto the truck bed, where the boys roll them to the back. Although girls pick potatoes through high school, teenage boys prefer working on a truck and in the potato house. At my section, Tommy jumps down grinning and with his big hands shovels potatoes into my basket. Lickety-split, it's full, dumped and refilled. He sticks one of my tickets onto the barrel and sets up another one. He stays until I have only the last two rows to pick, then leaps back onto the truck on its return trip.

"I wish Daddy could pick potatoes with me," I tell Mary Ann one day.

"You shouldn't wish for that," Mary Ann says. "Your father is in a hospital. Picking potatoes wouldn't be good for him."

I don't argue with her. Daddy isn't in the kind of hospital she's thinking of.

My pay from the Miller farm adds up to enough for Mumma to take me to the Houlton Savings Bank on Market Square and open an account. This is a practice that we'll follow through high school. The goal is to spend half my earnings on winter clothes and save half for my college education. I cross the Square with Mumma to the Chain Apparel and buy a winter coat, which I pay for with a check, filled out, signed and torn from its neat stack.

This is the heyday of agricultural production when Aroostook, the largest county east of the Mississippi, is producing more potatoes than any other one state. There will come a day when small-time farmers can no longer make a living, and the super-wide harvesting machines employed by the newly big-time farmers eliminate the need for school kids. I grow up thinking that pickin' — we don't say "harvest" — is an Aroostook tradition, that for generations schools have let out from the end of September to mid-October so that the students, whether or not they're farm kids, can help the farmers and earn money to buy winter clothes and build savings accounts. I'm surprised when Mumma tells me that isn't so. "It started during the Second World War," she says. "When there weren't enough men to work on the farms. And it's continued ever since." She, herself, Mumma tells me, picked potatoes only once. She worked for a farmer with a balky horse — this was before the advent of tractors. At one point the farmer became so exasperated he picked up a sizable rock and heaved it at the horse. Missing its mark, it struck my mother in the head. "Oh, my God," Mumma quotes the farmer shouting, "I've killed her." That was the only day Mumma ever picked potatoes.

One day a man phones Aunt Celia and says, "Are you Clement's mother?"

"Is he all right? Has anything happened?" Aunt Celia asks. The man explains that he's looking for boys to deliver *The Bangor Daily News,* and Celia gives him our number.

When my mother answers the phone, he says, "Are you Clement's mother?"

"Is he all right?" Mumma shouts into the phone. "Has anything happened?"

Clement gets a paper route. Six mornings a week he slings a canvas bag filled with folded papers over his shoulder, walks up to the end of our street and across the bridge to his route. Saturday afternoons he retraces the route, knocking on doors to collect the money. Sometimes I help with the folding or delivering or collecting, but mostly it's his job.

Don Moran, the man who recruited him for the job, comes one evening a week to settle accounts. Tall and slim with male-pattern balding, a five-o'clock shadow and a nice way with kids, he sits at the kitchen table with Clement, Charlie and me, sorting and counting coins. Don Moran talks about dates and mints; he collects silver pennies, and for a while Clement does, too. Clement gets to keep some — eventually all — of what he earns, but that first year half goes to Mumma for household use, as does half the money Tommy earns at odd jobs. (Or maybe Tommy had a paper route as well — I don't remember. And maybe it was the second year I picked potatoes that half was set aside for college. Perhaps that first year all of our modest wages went towards warm clothing.)

A year or so later, the *Bangor Daily News* runs a contest for the paperboys. Those who add a certain number of subscribers, get to go on a trip to the Ice Capades in Boston. Rising to the challenge, Grampa helps Clement extend his route and initially drives him around it in the mornings. Clement is a winner. He returns from the trip all aglow and with a miniature golden paperboy in a snow globe, which Mumma sets atop the bookcase that holds the *Encyclopedia Americana*. Grampa retires from chauffeuring in the mornings, and Clement is left with a very heavy bag and a very large route for a young boy.

As long as order prevails, Grampa enjoys the bustle of a busy household. "Meals at all hours and horses to let," he cheerfully quotes from the motto of a bygone inn whenever company drops in. He still gets along better with Mumma, Charlie and me than with my older brothers, but they're too busy with their own pursuits and too well brought up to challenge him openly. "Tommy makes friends with any Tom, Dick or Harry," Grampa once complained to Mumma in Woolwich. "Tartars," Grampa dubs some of Tommy's Houlton friends. Clement, too, takes up with boys from St. Mary's that let the door slam and are too rowdy or goofy or aimless for Grampa's taste. "That boy acts like a monkey," he says of a new friend Clement brings home. Grampa's much more accepting of my friends, whose indoor behavior is calm and sweet. Maybe Grampa just prefers girls to boys; maybe he enjoyed his own daughters more than he did his sons. At any rate, I am his obliging companion and, even though I miss Daddy every day, Grampa has begun to seem like a father to me. So that we learn the value of both bounty and thrift, he gives Charlie and me a weekly allowance; mine is fifty cents.

Grampa himself is a model of thrift and bounty. He slices up extra cabbage from the garden and soaks it in a blue and grey crock full of brine which he stows behind the kitchen stove where it bubbles and hisses like Snap, Crackle and Pop. Sauerkraut is too strong in both taste and smell for us kids to eat much of but there's plenty if we want it and Grampa and Mumma appear to relish it. He buys ice cream by the five-gallon tub, several flavors at a time, and keeps it in the shed in a chest freezer along with a goodly supply of frozen garden vegetables and roadside berries.

Grampa drives us out into the countryside to gather apples from abandoned orchards nearly swallowed up by woods. Errant hydrangeas, stove-in well houses, lopsided old barns and tiger lilies by crumbling foundations further attest to the migration from lumber and potato country to the factories of Massachusetts and Connecticut. Dimly, we kids know that someone pretends to ownership to every parcel of land in town, but unoccupied countryside we view as common property, the fiddleheads, berries, apples and Christmas trees rightfully owned by the first people to get to them. Grampa knows feral apples by name as well as where to find each variety as it comes into season. Little red crabapples look inviting, but, like chokecherries, are sour enough to make us wince. Grampa, adding a dash of pectin and a heap of sugar, will cook some up into jelly for us to spoon onto our breakfast toast. Sweet McIntoshes, which we consider the absolute best, we must eat within the few weeks before they soften. Tart, crunchy Northern Spies can be kept in our cool shed for months along with purple Spartans that will sweeten the longer they're stored. What we don't eat in the hand Grampa or Mumma will bake into pies and crisps. (When Mumma makes a pie, she cleans up after herself as she goes along. When Grampa takes over the kitchen, he brings every appliance and tool into play. Cupboard doors hang open and flour sifts into the open silverware drawer.)

For our intellectual nourishment, Grampa subscribes to *The Saturday Evening Post* and *Readers Digest*. In our home library, the books my mother grew up with, I read *Heidi* and feel well acquainted with Grandfather, his homey routines, the way he gives his orphaned granddaughter his undivided attention, the way he understands and anticipates her needs. I am drawn into *Black Beauty,* and *Beautiful Joe,* about a dog whose fortunes are as mixed as Black Beauty's, because both horse and dog seem as real as people or as my dolls and their frightful mistreatment as palpable. I have fellow feeling for Beauty, who spends his early life in the country with his gentle mother who teaches him, like my Mumma, to be kind to others. Older and out in the bigger world, he discovers, as I have, that others are not always kind nor circumstances idyllic. He remembers his mother's counsel, however, and aims to be his best no matter what, the way Sister Bernard and Sister Gemma remind their pupils that as Catholics and students at St. Mary's more is expected of us.

Beautiful Joe, like Aunt Celia's Meatball, is a homely mutt living in a small town in Maine, having been rescued from desperate circumstances by kindly humans. Joe proves to have a beautiful soul — if an animal can be said to possess a soul. Although my family doesn't have a dog, Meatball is almost as good as ours. Given the run of the neighborhood and having the good sense to return to Uncle George and Aunt Celia's for his meals, he often pooches around our yard, tail wagging, brown eyes adoring when he sees one of us kids, especially Clement, his former housemate. We don't lavish the attention on him Aunt Celia does, talking to him in a sweet, high- pitched tone. I don't see in him the wise observer that Beautiful Joe is. And yet, in a taken-for-granted kind of a way, we kids love Meatball.

As wise as Black Beauty and Beautiful Joe, Pollyanna sees the good in everyone. Although she's an orphan dependent on the charity of others, she has figured out how to talk herself into a good mood, and she teaches her technique, "the glad game," to the mopey adults who inhabit her village, a place I imagine looking like my home town as it might have been when my grandparents were children, the blacksmith shop on Mechanic Street one of many holdovers from that time.

Freckles and *A Girl of the Limberlost* take me far from town life and into a wilderness swampland I can satisfactorily imagine based on the tame strips of woods near houses I've lived in and fields I've picked in. Like me, Freckles is of Irish descent. Unlike me, he is an orphan who knows nothing about either parent. I have always been with Mumma; and Daddy, while not with us at present, is where I know him to be, the Augusta State Mental Hospital, and will surely return to us before too awfully long. At the story's end, Freckles, discovered by an uncle who had long sought him, finds that his parents, who had died in a fire, had loved him dearly and were of the Irish aristocracy. Turning down the opportunity to go to Ireland and live as a lord, he decides instead to attend college and then return to spend the rest of his life in the Limberlost — just as I would do. (My acquaintance with college life is limited to Mumma's copy of *Betty Wales, Freshman,* which, alluring as it makes college appear, I will eventually discover to be quaintly misleading and hopelessly out of date.)

Elnora, in *Girl of the Limberlost,* the sequel to *Freckles,* lives at the edge of the Limberlost. She's like Hansel and Gretel—*once upon a time at the edge of a great forest, there lived...* Only, in her case, she has no brother — or sister — and no father, just a mother who is as cold-hearted as Hansel and Gretel's stepmother. Other adults, kindly ones, come to her assistance the way my grandparents and aunts and uncles come to our aid, although Mumma isn't cold-hearted, only short on resources. As hard as Elnora's mother is toward her daughter, she remembers her dead husband with great fondness until confronted with evidence that he was unfaithful. Shocked by this news, she lets go of an idealized past and adopts a loving stance towards her daughter.

Adults are funny, I think, both terrible and wonderful, the terrible and wonderful sometimes all mixed up in one individual. As Sister says about people, each of these fictional adults has a cross to bear. When it's hidden, the person is inclined to do terrible things. Once it comes to light, everyone softens up and love reigns. In books and in life, many adults are like Humpty Dumpty perched on a dangerously high wall, if not already fallen and cracked. Unlike in the nursery rhyme, it's possible to put Humpty back together again and each of the stories I read ends happily — the way our family's story will once Daddy comes home to us.

I cultivate a Cary Library habit. Each of the orange biographies that fill an entire shelf in the children's section recounts the childhood of a famous person, the last chapter concerning the subject's adult achievement, dutifully read but least interesting. Along with the saints we hear about at school, these adults became important people — doctors, scientists, inventors, statesmen, missionaries, martyrs, mystics — and I'm inspired as are my classmates to picture ourselves living saintly, heroic lives.

The day Sister has each of us say what we want to be when we grow up, we snigger when stolid James says he wants to be a truck driver.

Little House in the Big Woods opens up the entire Laura Ingalls Wilder saga, which I read over the course of a few years, Mumma zipping through each volume I finish. "The conversations are made up," Mumma says with the cheerful camaraderie of a fellow reader. "No adult could remember everything that was said in their childhood word for word." *Made up conversations* — this is a new idea for me when it comes to a book written *by* Laura Ingalls Wilder *about* Laura Ingalls Wilder.

From the big woods to the prairie to the banks of Plum Creek to the shores of Silver Lake, the Ingalls family moves more than we do. Just as they get used to one new place, Pa finds it getting overpopulated and, sitting Ma on his lap, sweet talks her into moving farther into untamed territory. I'm hoping that when Daddy comes home he won't want us to move again. I have mostly happy memories of Patten and Woolwich, but Houlton is the best yet and I'd like us to stay here forever.

"We think maybe Lavender's pink!" Tommy says. He's sitting at the kitchen table talking about his history teacher. Mr. Lavender, a young man "from away," expresses ideas that sound Communistic to teenagers in our bastion of small-business, farm-oriented Republicanism. Maybe, Tommy speculates, Lavender isn't just putting forth ideas. Maybe he's trying to convert his students. Relating all this to Mumma, Tommy is excited and talking fast — as excited and fast as he must be in class discussions, which, although they challenge his beliefs, thrill him. (The motto under his picture in the yearbook will be *I'd rather be right than President.*) Mumma is more measured and, although certainly not soft on Communism, gives Mr. Lavender the benefit of the doubt, telling Tommy that perhaps his teacher merely wants to stir up lively discussions.

Equally lively discussions take place in Mrs. Rich's English class. We younger kids listen to Tommy recreate the scene for

Mumma: what austere Mrs. Rich said about Lady Macbeth, how Tory or Francis or Mike — tartars all — meekly responded, how Tommy was able to say something that cracked Mrs. Rich's stern composure and made her laugh.

Tommy's high school life sounds as event-packed and dramatic as that of Archie and Veronica. When his man-child friends come to the house they call him plain "Tom" and take the stairs two at a time up to his room. Milfred, whom the other boys have nicknamed "Nitch," owns a jalopy, which they call the Nitchmobile and all cram into to ride around town. Not much of a student, Nitch is a gifted artist. One day he shows the other boys a beautifully executed poster advertising an upcoming dance at the Rec Center. "Nitch," one of the boys says, "you should spell out the whole name of the Rec."

"What's that?"

"Rectum."

Pleased with the correction, Nitch tacks up the poster at the Rec, where it remains only briefly before the director snatches it off the wall.

The year before, at the Wednesday night Confraternity of Christian Doctrine classes held at St. Mary's Church, Tommy met Dina — sounds as though spelled with an "h" at the end — two years behind him in school and now his girlfriend. Dina's parents, of Franco-American background and suspicious of Irish Tom's interest in their daughter, curtail the time the two spend together. Mumma has reservations as well. A sophomore now, Dina is in Home Economics — a track composed largely of winsome girls who marry young — and although clever in the domestic arts, she shows very little intellectual promise compared to Tommy. Mumma doesn't want to see their young lives derailed by puppy love. To me, Tommy is as much in love with Dina as Archie is with Veronica, and I just know their love will prevail.

A more pressing concern for the family is what Tommy will do after high school graduation. Will it be possible for us to scrape together the money to send him to the University of Maine, where he would study engineering, a promising field, all the family agrees, for a smart young man? Is it possible Congressman Bill Hathaway will appoint him to West Point? Tommy isn't keen on becoming a soldier but our family doesn't see how he could pass up the free tuition.

Meantime, Tommy carries more authority at home than any of us younger kids. Always Mumma's champion, he permits not the slightest disrespect towards her from us. Evenings he makes fudge, trying out many varieties — chocolate, peanut butter, and divinity, a favorite for its white, whipped airiness. Sometimes he makes popcorn. One evening he makes both fudge and popcorn, stirs them together, lets the mess harden and breaks it into lumpy pieces to serve to us younger kids. One day he borrows Grampa's car with us younger kids in it. He picks up various friends of his and drives out to the Bangor Road, where he floors it and, for the first time in my life, I see a speedometer register ninety.

The kitchen table is where most family conversations take place. Aside from Sunday dinner and my mother's letter writing, the dining room table is for board games. Clement, Charlie and I often keep a game of Monopoly going through the week, playing after lunch and supper. When we ask Mumma to join us, she says, "No. That's why I had four children; so you'd have each other to play with." Clement usually wins and doesn't try to hide his glee. For Charlie and me, it's one long lesson in good sportsmanship, although Charlie is just quirky enough a player to be unsettling. (A few years later, when Tommy and Clement teach him poker, they're so thrown off by his unpredictable plays and consummate poker face that they're tempted to think he's cheating.) Once towards the end of a marathon game of Monopoly when it becomes apparent that there's no way I won't win, Clement half stands, reaches across the table and runs his hand over the board, scattering the pieces. We exchange a knowing look, satisfaction enough for me — he has avoided the humiliation of an official loss but we both know that for once I've bested him.

Outside the house, Clement, Charlie and I each make separate friends in this treasure town of playmates, our very own hometown, Houlton. My own friendships are blossoming. After school and weekends, I often play with Ann and Mary and Cobina and my other classmates. Mary Ann's mother starts a Girl Scout troupe for fifth, sixth and seventh graders. We meet in her living room, and I see where Mary Ann gets her energy and flair.

Mary Ann has made friends with another Mary Ann, this one a seventh grader, and I am welcomed into a triumvirate. Mary Ann Bartinoski and I walk together across town to where Mary Ann McDonald lives in a roomy house set in a neatly landscaped yard. She has a brother in high school and two sisters who've graduated. She also has a sister Barbara only one year younger than I, but I am no more interested in her than I am in Carol, Mary Ann Bartinoski's sister who is two years younger than I. Once upon a time when we lived in Woolwich and Charlie and his age-mate Debby were the only children within walking distance, I had enjoyed being the oldest and taking charge — up to a point. Now Houlton offers me girls my age and, most satisfactorily, girls even older than I, all of whom want to be my friend. I'm not inclined to bother with littler kids.

The two Mary Anns and I decide to start a club. Mary Ann Bartinoski and I agree that it should be run by majority rule; Mary Ann McDonald dissents. "But it's two against one for majority rule," Mary Ann Bartinoski says.

"We don't have majority rule," Mary Ann McDonald says, "because I haven't voted for it."

Baffled by this precocious preference for consensus, we don't get any farther in our plans for a club. When the three of us play together, however, it's the McDonald home where we gather. When just Mary Ann Bartinoski and I get together, we play in the clubhouse we've put together in her basement. There, Mary Ann takes charge of our activities and we find no need for majority or any other rule.

One day at the McDonalds, Mary Ann's sister Jeanne invites us into her bedroom. Slight and pretty, Jeanne has returned home because she's had a "nervous breakdown," a term I'm familiar with. Jeanne's time isn't taken up with friends or work or study or much of anything I can see except chain smoking. Since she doesn't seem to leave the house, ever, she's always there when we are, sometimes ignoring us, other times treating us as equals. This day, sitting on the edge of her bed, she pulls out a cigarette, then proffers us the pack, clinching for me the thought that Jeanne McDonald, a woman in her twenties blithely offering cigarettes to a ten, eleven and twelve year old, is not of sound mind. Mary Roach's mother often sits with us girls in her living room, smoking and making conversation, but she doesn't ever hold the pack out to us. But, then, Mrs. Roach hasn't had a nervous breakdown.

Suddenly, I'm picturing my family at the top of our Woolwich driveway bidding goodbye to a car full of people — maybe one of Mumma's old Colby "chums" or someone distantly related to us — who'd spotted the *McGillicuddy Florist* sign on their way up or down Route One and dropped in to call. This happened every once in a while, and Daddy, once or twice for the amusement of the departing company and in spite of Mumma's protestations, would let me take a puff off his cigar. Then I remember a behavior of Mumma's that happened more than once and made us kids laugh every time. Holding onto the open car window, she'd lean in talking faster and faster about topics she wanted to cover before the company was gone for good. When the driver started the ignition, she'd walk, then run, alongside until the car picked up speed and she had to let go. "Mumma's running away!" we kids would crow. (Thank God Almighty she never did.)

I wonder how Daddy's coming along at the Augusta State Mental Hospital. Will he be strange like Jeanne McDonald? I don't think so. I've never noticed Daddy acting crazy. If anyone, it's Mumma who can look a little crazy, especially if she's excited and forgets to modulate her voice and begins exclaiming. "Don't exclaim," Daddy used to tell her. "You're exclaiming." That time we vacationed in Bar Harbor and on other travels, sometimes Mumma would be at a little distance from the rest of us and we'd hear her suddenly exclaim with delight. "She must have met someone from Colby," Daddy would say, himself at that moment a paragon of self-possession. After his stay at the Augusta State

Mental Hospital he will no doubt be better than ever. In a few months I'll see for myself because Daddy, Mumma tells us, might be coming home for Christmas.

10

Winter 1953-54 and Spring

"Car, car, C.A.R!" I'm at the top of the hill on River Street, which glistens with a couple of inches of packed, slick snow. As I call out the alert to those on sleds down below, I pull my own sled into the snowdrift and stand aside for a vehicle that approaches from further up the street. Snow has arrived for the season, and River Street is a favorite sliding spot for kids from our street and the surrounding ones. In the barn, Clement, Charlie and I have found old sleds, which we tie new ropes to. We find also an assortment of cracked black leather skates and two toboggans. Tommy creates a toboggan path starting at the street, down our driveway, over the precipitous rise in front of the garden and alongside the river into the woods. Toboggans aren't easy to steer and are better for a whole family of kids to crowd onto than for a child alone to try to navigate. Tommy gives us a running push, then stands or kneels on the end, pulling on the reins and shouting for us to lean right or left. If we lean too far one way or if we hit a bump we all go tumbling off, soft snow grazing our faces, crusty chunks chafing and chilling our wrists suddenly exposed between mitten and jacket cuff. We roll over in a heap, jump up and run after the toboggan, which, skimming along lightly without us, heads for the river.

Trucks dump snow onto the level area left by the demolished armory and snowplows push it back into banks along the side. Each winter over the next few years, Clement, Charlie and I build a network of tunnels into these snowbanks. Clement builds the most and his are the most elaborate. One is an iced tube in which we slide from the top of the bank to the bottom. When the snow is deepest we look for a high place to jump off into it. Freddie's garage is a good height, but, for reasons we can't fathom, his grandparents forbid our jumping from it. One evening after supper, Clement, Charlie and I climb out the window of the boys' bedroom onto the roof and around to where the snow has heaped up outside the kitchen. Clement does a flip, executing a full turn in the air, and Charlie and I follow in rapid succession, going straight down. We all land in the snow up past our waists, our boots tightly wedged. At once there's a frantic rapping at the window behind us, where Mumma is washing dishes — and where by rights we should be helping her. She motions us in and forbids us to ever jump from the roof again, and we never do — not, at least, when she's looking.

Some afternoons, we hang our tied skates around our necks and walk up to the end of River Street and into the fairgrounds to the town skating rink. Overhead lights keep the rink operating through the short, dark afternoons and early evenings. The "shack" is an actual shack with a wood-burning stove in the middle of the floor. A record player pumps music out to the rink, where the games of crack the whip are fiercer than anything Gershwin Trot ever executed. Boys prevail in this game. If the whip gets so big it threatens to take over the whole rink or if the injuries pile up and begin to look life-threatening, an adult intervenes.

On a clear evening once this winter and every once in a while in the following winters, we kids stand aside in amazement and admiration to watch an older couple glide arm in arm around the rink in time to a waltz. They are dancing on ice! And we know them. It's Ann's parents, Mr. and Mrs. Caldwell.

Skating and tobogganing are fun, but "sliding" — as we call sledding — is right outside our door and requires the least expertise. On school days, by the time we get home, eat a snack and change into snowsuits, it's already getting dark. As one of the oldest in the crowd, and because it's my street, I command a certain authority over the others. Since swearing is never heard in my house, I extend the prohibition to the street. We put hours in on sliding. If we want more of a challenge, we turn right at the top of River Street hill and pull our sleds to the top of the short, steep rise that is Orchard Street. We stay out until our feet are numb, our faces burnt by wind and cold and drifting snow, our mittens festooned with rhinestones of ice. Clement lasts longest out in the cold. Once, when we lived in Patten, he was out sliding when the runner of another child's sled shot into his mouth and out his cheek. Anesthetized by the cold, he continued to slide for the rest of the afternoon. When he got home, Mumma saw the extent of his injury but also that the cold had sealed it and nothing more had to be done, although he was to retain the scar for the rest of his life. A more alarming incident with Clement occurred in Patten when Mumma looked out our living room window to see a logging truck overtake him on his sled. Luckily, the sled had passed between the wheels and he was safe in the ditch on the far side of the street.

Once inside, we kids crowd around the forced hot-air register, careful not to shock our cold feet with too much of a contrast, which Mumma and Grampa warn will lead to chilblains, that bumpy, itchy inflammation of feet, hands or ears that each of us gets a touch of at least once a winter.

Winter has only begun when Mumma tells us Daddy's coming home for Christmas for sure — and most likely for good. We haven't seen him since last Christmas. He and Mumma exchange weekly letters, but she doesn't tell us much about what his says — or hers either, for that matter. Mumma never lies to us kids, not even little white lies. It's as if something in her won't let her do that. In Woolwich, when Clement and Charlie and I played hide and seek in the house on rainy days, if I asked, *Did he go that way?* she'd say nothing rather than deceive. On subjects that make her uncomfortable she clams up and we know better than to try to pry her open, but she never, never fabricates. So, although we sense a limit to how much she'll reveal, we know that anything she does tell us about Daddy is true.

Often in the evening after supper, before pushing the extensions back into the maple table and moving it against the wall, we kids and Mumma linger, recounting all the good times we had with Daddy. Slowly, the stories take form, Mumma or Tommy filling in gaps for us younger kids: the time in Patten when Daddy put on a Halloween party in the town hall so the youth wouldn't run amok all over town smashing eggs and puncturing tires; the time he gave the boys their haircuts and saved the money to take us all to Bar Harbor; the time — my favorite memory — he took me, because I begged to be included, on a hike up Haystack Mountain with Tommy and Clement and how, true to my promise, I walked uncomplainingly all the way up and all the way down even though Clement gave out half way down and Daddy had to carry him. Daddy's the star in all the stories.

Now Daddy is coming home. This isn't like the first time he had a breakdown and when he returned I didn't know him from Uncle George. I remember what he looks like. Still, he's been away for a long time, and much has changed. We don't even live in Woolwich anymore. When we lived in Patten, when we younger kids were little, if he was left in charge of us for an evening, he would comb his pompadour down over his eyes, stoop over letting his arms dangle, cry, "I'm the big, bad gorilla" or "I'm the big bad wolf," and chase us shrieking upstairs and down. He'd sit me on his knee and rub his stubbly cheek against my tender one to make me giggle. When our family went grocery shopping on Saturdays, he gave me a nickel and a dime, an allowance meant to last all week but which I spent immediately on bubblegum and candy. Clement and I would stop into the town hall on our way home from school and run up the stairs into his office, where his secretary would be so happy to see us and he would open the safe and give us each a nickel or dime. Once, he led us down into the basement to show us the two jail cells where inebriated men were sometimes kept overnight. Another time, he and I were walking down Main Street when the fire truck came along, and Daddy took my hand and we jumped up onto the back and rode out into the country to the fire, which only amounted to a pile of stinking rubber tires a miscreant had poured kerosene on and set a match to. One late evening, a couple of older girls, sisters, came to the door to say there was no food in their house, and Daddy put on his hat and coat and went with them to see what he could do.

We kids were all much younger in Patten. Charlie lugged around a big fuzzy stuffed animal; Tommy created minor explosions with his chemistry set; Clement ate every meal using a knife, fork, and spoon that fit into its own leather kit, a birthday gift from Aunt Mary Vose. Charlie, too young to be expected to behave in church, stayed with our next door neighbors when the rest of us went to Mass. Clement and I would start out all right, but part way through we'd lose interest and begin to climb about on the kneelers. One such Sunday, Daddy drove us all out into the countryside where he pointed out a "spanking place," where children who didn't behave in Mass would be taken. We promised to be good. The following Sunday we forgot our promise and once again crawled around at Mumma and Daddy's feet. After Mass, Daddy drove out to the spanking place. While he was spanking me, Clement ran off into the woods. I returned to the car embarrassed by Mumma and Tommy's smirks. When Daddy and Clement got back, Daddy assured me that Clement, because he ran away, got the harder licking. It wasn't commonplace for us kids to get spanked, and I don't remember ever being spanked again. In Patten we kids had been very young.

Even Daddy and Mumma acted younger. Mumma chewed gum in Patten. After she'd chewed the sweetness out of a piece, she'd take it from her mouth to discard but then give it to me if I asked for it. Smoother and blander than the bubble gum I spent my allowance on, her gum retained the warmth and softness that was a part of her. Then, one day, she announced that she wasn't going to chew gum anymore because she felt she had a tendency to get carried away and make a show of herself chewing with her mouth open and snapping the gum. And she never did chew gum again. One April Fool's Day, a neighbor child said to Mumma, "There's a hole in your dress!" Mumma shrieked and turned to Daddy and threw her arms around his neck and he hugged her close, both of them laughing. Once, on a family picnic when my Uncle Ned was visiting, the men drank beer. More than once in winter, Daddy drove our car onto frozen Peavey Pond, my mother crying, "Oh, Joe," more in excitement than admonishment.

Woolwich made our family all older, and now, since last Christmas, the last time we saw Daddy, we kids are even more grown up. We tramp into the woods where Tommy chops down a tree that looks good *in situ* but rather pitiful transferred to our living room. I don't remember the Christmas of 1953 as well as the one before, the first time Daddy came home before being taken away from us again. I got a doll, I'm sure, because I asked for and got a doll every Christmas even after Mumma would question whether maybe I hadn't outgrown dolls. (I get a doll until about seventh grade when all my friends are mad about stuffed animals. That year I ask for and get a black plush dog I name Cinders, but in my heart of hearts I would really have preferred another doll, and the stuffed animals, meant as segue to more mature tastes, never displace dolls in my affections.)

Grampa prepares to spend Christmas at the home of another of his children. For presents to take with him, he makes caramel candy and popcorn balls. The candy is a fussy project involving hefty supplies of heavy cream and sugar and the use of a candy thermometer to determine the precise moment at which the bubbling mixture achieves the proper consistency. Grampa places individual pieces onto cut-up squares of wax paper, folds the paper and twists the ends. When it comes to the popcorn balls, we kids roll up our sleeves, wash our hands, and help press the popcorn and molasses mixture into sticky balls that dry as slick as plastic.

For the second Christmas, we sit at Daddy's feet and watch him unwrap his gifts, his presence and his presents the highlight of the day. His gift from Nana is a black and red checked lumberman's jacket, the biggest present of all. He'll need it. Mumma says he's staying with us in Houlton for good. Charlie leads him into the boys' room and points proudly to the cot in the corner of that room that's his. Daddy is now in the marriage bed with Mumma. Because the small front bedroom is Grampa's, there's no other place for my cot except their room.

On the weekends Daddy goes for long walks. We kids follow him up the street and out into the country. Lost in his own thoughts, he does nothing to encourage us. I can tell he wishes we'd leave him alone. We walk way out away from town. We come to a railroad track and follow that until we come to a trestle. Daddy strains to look ahead and seeing no train coming, starts across. We hesitate — you're not supposed to walk across trestles — then we follow him, ready to run like the dickens if we hear a locomotive's whistle. At midpoint, struck by how far we are from safety at either end, we freeze. Daddy stops and looks back at us. He seems to come to himself, to realize fully for the first time that we are there with him. "It's all right," he says. "Just keep moving. All you have to do is put one foot in front of the other." He stretches out his hands and we take them and we all get across and no train comes on this, after all, rarely used track.

Another time we tramp so far out into the country that I become exhausted on the return trip and say I can't go on. Once again, Daddy gives me his complete attention. "One foot in front of the other," he says. "All you have to do is put one foot in front of the other." He takes my hand and matches his step to mine, and one foot at a time we walk back to civilization. Even then, it occurs to me that "one foot in front of the other" is something he learned at Augusta State Mental Hospital. And, also, that putting one foot in front of the other is how he's living his new life. We kids are bigger now. We've changed. Has Daddy changed? If so, who is he now? The Lone Ranger rides into town and performs marvelous deeds. Then he rides away again. As the citizens stand watching him leave, one of them says, *Who was that masked man?* Now that the doctors at the Augusta State Mental Hospital have given Daddy back to us, we want to get to know him again.

Our family spends a Sunday afternoon with our uncles and aunts and cousins at Uncle Paul's woods camp on the side of a road in a territory so sparsely inhabited it goes only by the name B Plantation. Short on the cutting and filling that even River Street exhibits, the hills on these back roads provide heart-stopping thrills. Daddy takes the lead as we drag toboggans and sleds to the top. Speaking of him and his brothers and sisters, Mumma has said that they never forgot what it's like to be children, and, indeed, on this outing and the ones that follow, Daddy stays out with us after dark, while my uncles get a good fire going in the pot-bellied stove and my mother and the aunts prepare supper.

Since Daddy doesn't yet have a car of his own, Grampa McGillicuddy sometimes appears on a Sunday afternoon to take us all for a ride around town and out into the country. One Sunday a woebegone little neighbor boy, about four years old, stands by watching us pile in. "I think there's room in that big car for me," he says aloud but to no one in particular. When this child goes out to play his mother, we know, locks the door behind him and he's not let back in until the end of the afternoon when she's finished her housework or whatever it is she spends her time doing.

"Let him in," Grampa says. "We'll get him an ice cream to wash his face with."

Daddy goes to work. For a brief stint he shovels coal and comes home at the end of each day his eyes and lips shining out of a face blackened with coal dust. Another job is driving a bakery truck from Houlton to the airbase sixty miles north in Limestone. Clement, Charlie and I walk with him after supper to the bakery yard to load the truck. We take home some of the pastries and end the evening with the whole family snacking at the kitchen table, cream puff lard coating the roofs of our mouths so thickly we can peel it off with our fingernails. On Saturdays, we kids take turns riding on the truck with Daddy. As we drive along, Daddy doesn't relate family sagas the way Mumma does, but he does make allusions to his childhood. On the farm, Daddy says as we pass below Littleton Ridge where the McGillicuddys lived before they moved to town, there would sometimes pop up an odd creature who was the cross between a cat and a rabbit. "It wouldn't know whether to eat grass or chase mice," Daddy says, shaking his head over the misfit's sad conundrum. Daddy talks about the small towns we pass through: Monticello, which he calls "Monkey-Say-Hello;" Mars Hill, its main street of false fronts like the set for a Western movie; Blaine, named after a governor who ran for President and lost because he failed to respond to the charge of "Rum, Romanism and Rebellion;" Presque Isle, which Daddy calls "Preskey Whizzle."

Uncle Paul hires Daddy to do odd jobs. One Saturday, Daddy packs a lunch of his own devising and, taking Clement, Charlie and me with him, drives to Uncle Paul's lakeside camp — "camp" being the word for secondary dwellings ranging from hovels to handsome summer homes. As we travel south on twisty Route One, Clement is the only one of us kids who remembers milestones along the road. "Look," he says. "We're going to run right into that barn." And so it seems until the road takes a sudden sharp turn. In Amity, at the foot of a steep hill, we pass by an abandoned two-story building, which, Daddy says, was the home where above the general store and post office — his mother was postmistress — he was born.

We arrive at Grand Lake. My memory of the camp itself goes back to the week we spent here right after Daddy returned from his first hospitalization. I remember running and hopping barefoot alongside Mumma through a thistly field to buy milk from a nearby farm. I remember us all in Uncle Paul's boat, Baby Charlie in a basket in the bottom and Tommy and Clement setting up a rocking motion to make me cry until Mumma and Daddy made them stop. I remember the smell of gasoline rainbows on the water, of sooty kerosene lamps and crackling wood fires. When we lived in Patten, our family used to drive over to the lake sometimes to spend a day. This day the camp's all closed up. After Daddy turns off the gas or sets the mouse traps or whatever it is he's been sent there to do and gleefully unpacks the lunch, his face drops. He's forgotten the filling for our sandwiches. "Holy limpin' lightnin' Ponto!" Then his face brightens. "That's okay," he says. "We'll have jam sandwiches."

"Where's the jam, Daddy?" Clement asks, a little suspiciously.

"You just take two pieces of bread," Daddy holds up two pieces. "And you jam them together!" He claps the bread together, eyes it with relish and takes a big bite. Clement laughs, and we kids make jam sandwiches of our own. When he puts his mind to it, Daddy can make anything fun.

Although Daddy can be great company, making up words and off-beat explanations, he's often distracted, as though his thoughts are a million miles away, allowing him no leisure to pay attention to us kids or to join in the care of us or in the ordinary tasks of family life. When he does zero in, he's like an attentive, playful uncle — a visiting uncle, with us for a short time before going off again, although where Daddy goes off to is not a geographical location but a place inside his own head.

One day in the spring of 1954, when run-off from the winter's snow has swollen the river and flooded our garden, Charlie stands in the yard watching a rowboat with two fishermen in it pass under the bridge. Suddenly the boat flips over, pitching the men into the raging current. For the next few days our driveway and yard fill up not only with rescue workers and their vehicles but also with spectators. Although Mumma feels bad for the drowned men and their families, she's not happy about our place being turned into a spectacle. When one and then more of the gawkers knock on our kitchen door to ask to use the bathroom, she's abrupt in her refusal. "Isn't that the limit!" she fusses to us kids.

One of the drowned men was the father of my classmate Earl, a tall, thin, quiet boy with a pale face and freckles. Like most of my classmates, he looks enough like my family to be a relative, but we're not actually blood relatives. We don't live near each other and except for Sunday Mass I hardly ever see him outside of school, and when he returns to school after the funeral I never hear him mention his father. But ever after, whenever I look at

Earl I think: *his father is gone and will never come back.* And I know that I am very lucky to have my Daddy back.

Except that now, it seems, I have two fathers under one roof, and that's one too many.

11

Divided Loyalties

At St. Mary's School, the parents of quite a few of our classmates have emigrated from Canada and become naturalized citizens of the USA. We tease these kids by saying "civilized" for "naturalized" and asking them if they plan to attend "Old Home Week," an annual fair in our sister town of Woodstock, New Brunswick. The funny thing is that almost all of us with Irish surnames have at least one grandparent who came from Canada, our forebears having got to the New World via the shortest, cheapest route. The ancestors of the French in our midst fled Nova Scotia. The Indians are citizens of both countries. Perhaps, paradoxically, it's the very geographic and genealogical proximity to another sovereign nation that makes us feel so proud to be Americans. (Years later I will realize that many of the Protestant friends I make at Houlton High School have Loyalist ancestors whose descendants recrossed the border.)

"Canadians are Americans, too," Mumma says. "People from the United States and people from Canada, we're all Americans."

"During the Revolution," Daddy says, snatching at the air, "we should have made a grab for Canada."

Ann and I are walking down Charles Street exchanging catty remarks about fellow students at St. Mary's School — the one who plays the piano with no expression, the one who shows off with expensive outfits. Then Ann says something derogatory about Clement. Without a word, I turn on my heel and head off in the other direction. Ann has done this before, criticized Clement, and I know she wouldn't mind a bit if I reciprocated with a snide comment about Peter, but then she and her brother have never been separated for the better part of a year and, by the grace of God, reunited. Although there's not much I can do the following year whenever Sister Bernard, Charlie's teacher, passes me in the hall, shakes her head and says, "That Charlie will be the death of me," I will not tolerate criticism of my family by someone my own age. My drop-dead performances impress Ann sufficiently for her to stop bringing Clement into our conversations. (What was killing Sister Bernard, by the way, was that instead of following each lesson along with the rest of the class, Charlie read from whatever of his books struck his fancy. One day, Sister took all his books out of his desk and placed them on a far windowsill, returning to him one at a time the book the class was presently working from. Later, when she called on him to recite, she saw that his desk was empty and that he was sitting on the windowsill immersed in a book of his choice.)

One day a test comes between an irresistible force and an immovable object. "Yes, you will," Clement says.

"No, I won't," Mary Ann says.

"Will."

"Won't."

Clement says he won't swerve his bike. (Or was it his sled? Memory fails.) Mary Ann says she won't move aside. My heart is in my mouth. I know the word "kamikaze" from comic books and I know Clement's kamikaze ways. Years later Tom will tell me that he had to finish a lot of Clement's battles because the younger brother would start a fight with someone bigger and stronger and take a licking, leaving it up to the older brother to salvage family honor. If we kids are left at home on our own for any length of time, Clement, although he and his brothers are fiercely devoted to each other, is apt to rebel against Tommy's authority until a fistfight ensues. One day one of them threw the other against the kitchen cabinets, shattering one of the glass fronts. I know that if Clement comes down the hill on his bike he won't alter his course to avoid someone perfectly capable of getting out of the way. I know him.

I also know Mary Ann. Tall, pretty, blonde, oldest child in her family, a Girl Scout, devisor of our elaborate games of dress up, she has an unshakable belief in her rights — and of other people's obligation to honor those rights.

Clement turns around and pushes his bike to the top of the hill. Mary Ann stands in the middle of the street at the bottom. I would give anything for this madness to stop, for a never-ending line of cars to appear, for our mothers to call us in to eat, for lightning to come out of the sky and blast the roadway to smithereens. Clement mounts his bike and aims full speed at Mary Ann. As he comes closer and closer, he fully expects her to move aside while she fully expects him to swerve. The crash is awful. Mary Ann's face spurts blood. Clement's is stricken. He and I help her to her feet and into her house. Her mother sits her down and pats at her face with a wet washcloth and applies iodine. A hearty soul who lets one child commandeer the basement and another dig an endless pit in the front yard, she assumes an accident and doesn't press for details or try to assign blame. And neither Clement nor Mary Ann nor I, chastened as we all are, explain what happened.

Daddy is always polite to Grampa but behind his back he makes fun of him, the humor ranging from good-natured to mean-spirited. When Mumma gets up in the night to go to the bathroom and passes the open door of Grampa's bedroom, and Grampa calls out, "Who's there?" Mumma doesn't answer because she doesn't hear him. When it's Daddy who passes Grampa's door, he doesn't answer because, as he tells us kids, he doesn't have to give an accounting of himself in his own house. When Daddy says his belly is not his god, we know he's casting aspersions on Grampa, who loves to cook and eat and talk about food and who also has a big belly. "You-whaaa?" Daddy says, laughing, in imitation of Grampa, who, although not exactly hard of hearing like Mumma, is losing acuity due to his advanced age, "you, what?" being his frequent call for us to repeat what we've said.

Grampa drives to Pennsylvania to spend a few weeks with Aunt Ruth and Uncle Norman. He writes that he will be back on a particular Monday. Soon after, Daddy sees a newspaper ad for a movie called "Black Monday" and he employs that title to refer to Grampa's return. We are all in the kitchen one day when Daddy's teasing about Black Monday goes beyond Mumma's endurance.

"Shut up," she says.

For a long moment, no one speaks, no one moves. Mumma's standing in the middle of the kitchen, Daddy's at the doorway to the dining room facing her. "Shut up" is a term we kids aim at each other but never in the presence of our parents, and we have never heard either of them ever say such a thing to the other. We see Daddy trying to put a face on things by feigning shock — to cover up the shock he must really feel — and laughing politely. Then he walks to his chair in the living room, Mumma goes to the stove, and time resumes.

Grampa goes to live first in a rooming house and then an apartment because, really, we are too crowded, especially in the bedroom department. And now, I move into the front bedroom he's vacated. For the first time, I have a room of my own! Mumma helps me arrange it: on one side of the bed a small chest of drawers that was made for baby clothes, a vanity table on the other, a rocking chair and a full set of drawers next to the window, a small built-in closet all to myself with a drape where a door might be. Nothing new and all mismatched — eventually, I will paint everything a light pink, the walls, too — but for now I'm happy as it is.

In the night, in spite of the doll I sleep with, I feel lonely. I get out of bed and go through Mumma and Daddy's room into the boys' room. I lean over Charlie's cot and shake him awake. He dutifully follows me into my bed. This happens a few times but never works out satisfactorily because since we've moved from Woolwich, this bed has become too small for the two of us. Charlie has grown longer arms and legs and, truth to tell, so have I. Honestly, I'm more comfortable sleeping alone. With only my doll for company, I leave my door open and grow drowsy listening to Mumma and Daddy and my older brothers — Clement has never needed as much sleep as I do — walking around and talking downstairs, their voices rising up the stairwell into the hall next to my room. I am lying in a covered wagon in a caravan of covered wagons traveling westward. During much of the day, I walked and skipped alongside the oxen, sometimes running ahead to pick wildflowers. Now it's night and the wagons have been circled around a campfire, where some of our party are crouched, talking over the day's events and making plans for the morrow. Inside our snug wagon, my family in linsey-woolsey night clothes is nestled under patchwork quilts and bear skins. My baby clutched to my bosom, I drift off to sleep.

One Sunday, I leave the dinner table in tears because a loose tooth makes eating too painful. I go to my room. A few minutes after I lie down on my bed, Daddy comes in and sits on the side. "Just use your thumb and one finger and move the tooth one way very gently, then the other way," he says. "Push one way, then the other, one way, then the other." I do, gingerly, until after quite a few minutes the tooth's last mooring snaps, and I lift it out. Daddy and I go downstairs where I rinse my mouth and we sit down to eat the dinner Mumma has saved for us.

If Grampa Vose feels displaced, he doesn't act that way. Since our garden is now Daddy's, he locates a plot across town where he can plant the sort of weedy, messy business that he pays only half a mind to. He has cards printed up reading "Vose Collection Agency" and persuades businesses to give him the accounts in arrears that they're ready to give up on. As always, he plans each day as efficiently as a paper route. If I'm with him in the car to buy produce in, say, Littleton, we might go out of our way to call on a debtor on Littleton Ridge. On the floor of the back seat is a baseball bat, which Grampa takes out when he knows there's a fierce dog on the premises. One time, we stop in at a place after Mass, and the man of the house yells at Grampa, "It's against the law to dun on a Sunday! So, now I don't owe you nothin'!"

Grampa buys two season's tickets to the Community Concert Series that comes to Houlton during the winter season, and I am his companion. I haven't the talent to judge whether Grampa is musical, but as for myself, the concerts are a time to look around at the rest of the audience and to lose myself in daydreams with a backdrop of sound that makes me feel sad or dreamy or excited but which I don't really follow and couldn't possibly describe or reproduce with either an instrument or my voice. Intermission provides a welcome break for both Grampa and me, and he seeks out friends and acquaintances to chat with and purchases some of the homemade sweets for sale. By the final number, it's past his bedtime and he gestures for me to stop applauding, as though he and I alone could stem the tide of encores that more musical and less weary townsfolk are enthusiastically calling for.

As time goes by, it's just me who accompanies Grampa to the church suppers. In early summer we attend a "strawberry festival" at one congregation after another. I go with Grampa on the trips he makes around the state, calling on relatives and in-laws and taking in the odd bean-hole bean or community supper we see advertised in front of churches, town halls or fire stations. Once, we go out of our way to attend the Rockland Lobster Festival on the coast — all you can eat, chowder, rolls and corn on the cob included. There's nothing Grampa loves better than what he calls "a good feed." He buys produce at roadside stands as gifts for our host relatives and brings back to Houlton fruits and vegetables not yet in season in The County.

One relative we often call on is Cousin George, who lives in Waterville. He's Mumma's first cousin but because he's only about a year younger than Grampa, Mumma grew up calling him "Cousin," as it wouldn't be proper for a child to call an adult by his first name only. Cousin George is the oldest of the three children who came to live in Grampa's house after their mother died, and he and Grampa seem more like brothers than uncle and nephew. Except for one eyelid permanently closed after a childhood accident and a tattoo he regretted acquiring in the Navy, balding and portly Cousin George even looks like Grampa, but they're very different temperamentally. For one thing, Cousin George doesn't believe in religion. "Churches are places for hypocrites to hide," he once declared to my grandfather.

"Always room for one more, George," Grampa is said to have replied.

Cousin George is a widower and a retired liquor salesman. His wife Grace was an heir of the Lombard fortune — Lombard of caterpillar-tread renown. On the condition he not re-marry, Cousin George has the use of the money as long as he lives. Eventually, the inheritance will go to their son Alvin, who, according to Cousin George, conducts all his business poolside at his house in Los Angeles. Cousin George lives in the cavernous pink and grey basement of The Lombard, a mansion turned apartment building. There with him among the fine china and the leather armchairs and the mirrors advertising liquor lives an elegant, grey-haired woman named Lillian, who goes by no honorific at all, even for me, a child. The unusual situation of a man and woman living together without benefit of marriage is acceptable to my family due to the fact that they think it was mean of Grace to put such a stipulation in her will.

Like Grampa, Uncle George is an excellent cook, his meals very rich and tending more towards the gourmet. Like Aunt Ruth and Uncle Norman, he and Lillian drink cocktails before dinner. Cousin George is a big talker with strong opinions — Daddy has said he's a bigot — and he includes me in the conversation and tells jokes that are slightly risqué. "A little of George goes a long way," Grampa says, but after a few months go by he's always ready to see his nephew again.

We travel as far as Concord, New Hampshire, where Grampa's sister Nina lives. ("Nina" rhymes with "Dinah.") The bristles on Aunt Nina's upper lip tickle when she greets me with a kiss. She says the easiest thing is for me to sleep with her in her bed. In the morning she's out of sorts because apparently I kicked her all night long. Also, I hogged the covers and pulled the sheets out. "I'll have to remake the bed from scratch," she says. "Ordinarily I just have to smooth it up a little."

I'm a little embarrassed but say nothing, consoling myself with the thought that it was her idea for us to share a bed, not mine. She allocates me a bed to myself for the rest of the visit.

Aunt Nina is a widow — her husband Philip was the doctor uncle who tried so hard to find a remedy for Mumma's hearing loss. One of her two sons is also a doctor, practicing in New York City. Once, when he and his family visited us in Woolwich, some of us kids slept outside, and Daddy sprayed us with so much bug repellent my hair was soaking wet. Aunt Nina's other son, Henry, was a quiet, normal-appearing boy growing up, but somewhere in his teens he stopped talking and hasn't said a word since. He lives in some other part of Concord, and when he comes to visit it's with a man who has charge of him. This man talks; in fact, this man is loquacious and knows how to engage children in conversation. I like him.

I also like Aunt Nina's middle-aged boarder, Mary Brand. The fascinating thing about Mary Brand — and we don't comment on it in front of her — is that although she looks to me like anyone else, she's actually a Negro. She informed Aunt Nina of this fact before she moved in and said that if Aunt Nina objected she would look elsewhere, but my aunt said that she didn't object and that any friend of hers who did wasn't a true friend, a stance the family finds commendable.

In the car, Grampa explains about whatever town or countryside we're passing through — he can recite in alphabetical order the sixteen counties of Maine — and tells stories about the people we'll be visiting. Sometimes he tunes the radio to sentimental old songs and gets me to sing along with him. Other times he and I listen to preachers — a practice Clement frowns upon as they are invariably Protestant. Once, perhaps as a ploy to get me to stop talking so much, Grampa says, "I'll bet you a Dairy Joy you can't be silent for five minutes."

"Okay!" Having confused seconds with minutes, I shut my mouth and count to five. "Time's up. I win!" When Grampa corrects me, I start over, timing myself with the car clock, and am amazed at how difficult it is to remain silent for five whole minutes.

The second summer we're in Houlton and for a few summers following, Grampa makes a deal with a farmer to plant peas. Grampa supplies the seed, the farmer the field, and they divvy up the harvest. For a few weeks in early summer, Grampa drives Clement, Charlie and me to the field and leaves us there to work for a couple of hours. He shows us how to measure pecks and bushels into paper bags, discusses with us about how to price the bags, and drives us around to friends and acquaintances of his that he's solicited over the phone.

We enter the jewelry shop on Market Square. Behind the counter at the end of the long narrow shop sits Cedric Osgood, his bristly red head bent over a watch. He glances our way before continuing his work. After a few minutes he rotates the cylindrical eyepiece off his glasses and stands up. He rifles through the bag of peas which Clement has placed on the counter until he comes to one he holds up for our inspection. Dried out, wrinkled and a sickly shade of green, this overripe, end-of-season pod clasps its rock hard peas in a death embrace. Cedric Osgood glares at us as though we were a band of jewel thieves. Stricken, penitent, we say nothing in our own defense. He drops the pod back into the bag, opens the cash register and counts out into Clement's hand the price of the bag. We'll try not to let any overripe peas get into his next order — although, in spite of occasional lapses in quality control, week after week, year after year he keeps on buying, one of our most loyal customers.

Any bags left over, we sell bulk at a discount to the First National Grocery, a practice Clement prefers, as he finds peddling door to door, despite being more lucrative, slightly embarrassing. All the proceeds go to us kids. Grampa takes us into the Houlton Trust Company to open Christmas Club accounts.

On hot summer days, Aunt Celia's dog Meatball crosses River Street and ambles into our yard looking for a shady spot. One breathless day when we kids are lolling about the living room, we hear a shrill, rasping sound like metal being ripped apart. We run outside to see Meatball, who had the poor judgment to seek shade under Grampa's car, writhing *in extremis* on the driveway, Grampa standing by, a ghastly look on his face.

Clement whirls about, runs back inside and upstairs to his room. When he comes down some time later, his eyes are bloodshot and puffy. In answer to Mumma's solicitousness, he says he had not been crying and that, besides, he had never liked Meatball. Meatball's death, however, seems to add to Clement's resentment of Grampa — whose main fault all along has been that he's not Daddy. (Even so, Clement knows Grampa is someone who can be counted on. When in eighth grade the formidable Sister Albert asks if anyone's parents can help drive the class to Nickerson Lake for the June picnic, Clement volunteers Grampa. "You'll have to ask him first, Clement," Sister Albert says. "If I ask him," Clement says, "he'll do it.")

Grampa joins a rug hooking class at the Rec Center. Also a needlepoint class where he makes two pretty pictures of a boy and a girl to give to me. (Mum eventually gets them framed, and they hang in my house to this day.) The only man in the classes, he enjoys the attention of the ladies even though, Mumma says, he told her after Nana died that he would not be getting married again. At the rooming house, he meets Daisy, who becomes a "lady friend," in a most proper sense, not with an unconventional arrangement like Cousin George and Lillian's. Daisy has a sister Sarah — Daddy always refers to the two as "Pansy and Daisy" — who, we kids are amused to hear, is jealous of Grampa's attentions to her gentler, prettier sister. Grampa has plenty of friends and a knack for acquiring more.

He would like to be Daddy's friend. We kids can see that. What we also see is that what Daddy wants is to be free. What little he says about the Augusta State Mental Hospital over the next few years is that, unlike a prison sentence, once a person is placed in a mental hospital he never knows when or if he will be free again. Another time he says that he remembers shouting out a window over and over, "I was born in Amity, Maine, and amity means friendship." Sane, he's able to look back and see his insanity for what it was. (When in 1972 Thomas Eagleton, after his mental breakdowns and electric shock treatments are made public, withdraws as George McGovern's running mate, Dad will agree with the decision. "He could get sick like that again at any time," Dad says, "and then all you can think about is yourself.")

Daddy needs time to himself to remake his life. After he starts to work at the appliance store, Uncle Paul asks him to represent the business at the weekly Rotary luncheon meetings at the Northland Hotel. No sooner does this welcome task begin than Grampa dons his best suit with the fifty-year diamond pin from AT&T and joins Rotary himself. Daddy attends the Great Book Club at the library. Grampa does likewise. Entrenched courtesy to one's elders prevents Daddy from speaking up to Grampa, from telling or asking him not to dog his steps, to leave him alone, but at home we know from the caustic remarks he lets drop how frustrating Daddy finds Grampa's hovering presence.

Daddy tells us a story. When he and Mumma were first married, Uncle Clem, then still a boy, sometimes came to visit for a few days at a time. Once Daddy turned on his young brother-in-law and said, "Are you following me?" And, when the answer was in the affirmative, said, "Then stop it!" Always, privacy had contended with intimacy in the large family with children close in age that Daddy grew up in. "You're not the boss of me," is a childhood rejoinder Daddy quotes, laughing. Another is "What have you done for me lately?"

Although he tells only snippets, Daddy appears to remember his childhood well. Many of his adulthood memories, we kids know, have been blasted out of existence by electric shock therapy. The family stories we kids relate and the lore we get Mumma to tell are news to him. While we kids sit at the kitchen table with her after supper and talk about events pertaining to Sidney, Patten, Woolwich and also Houlton in earlier years, Daddy sits in his armchair in the living room, reading — and maybe listening. Sometimes, he leaves his chair and comes to the kitchen door, *Time* magazine dangling from one hand, his glasses from the other. The stories he hears us tell tickle him like the tales we kids enjoy hearing about ourselves as babies. Some please him so much he takes to telling them as though he remembers them first-hand — which we know he doesn't. "Remember the time in Patten," he'll say over the years with a big smile, "when I threw the Halloween party in the town hall so kids wouldn't get up to mischief."

Although I'm grateful for the electric shock therapy that quelled his demons sufficiently for him to return to us, I think now how disconcerting — terrifying, even — it must have been to have so much of his past blacked out. What are we without our memories? Who are we? No wonder he craved the freedom to find himself again, to make a new life.

12

Life Goes On

The Aroostook County economy depends on the potato crop. And the potato crop depends on the weather. Too much rain in the spring and the farmers can't plant; too much in the summer and the potatoes rot in the ground; not enough and they fail to thrive. In the fall, in good weather, the farmers spray their fields with poison to kill the tops and prepare for picking. If there's too much rain during picking, the school hiatus is extended a week and we pick on Saturdays, sometimes Sundays, too, to stay ahead of the first frost.

Through the seasons people greet each other with: "Nice day," "Looks like rain — the farmers could use it," "Aren't the leaves beautiful this year!" and "Enough snow for ya'?" Long distance telephone calls begin with "How's the weather down there?" as though the whole world were as dependent on a fierce, fickle climate as we are. We kids play outside in all weathers short of blizzards and forty below zero temperatures, when it's too cold even to snow. There's the weather overhead and the weather underfoot. Many a fine spring day overhead with blue skies and sunshine is treacherously muddy underfoot.

As dependent on the weather as any farmer are housewives, especially when it comes to laundry. A still, humid summer day can be worse for drying clothes than a short cold, dry winter day with a breeze. Ah, a good breeze that puffs the blouses and shirts, flaps the sheets and tablecloths! So often, however, the air is both wet and cold, either deadly still or nearly ripping the clothes off the line. Any one load of wash might go from the line outside to the semi-protected line on the back porch, back outside, back inside and ultimately to a collapsible wooden rack set next to the radiator. I'm Mumma's helper in the pinning up and shifting of laundry. To facilitate ironing, we acquire metal stretchers which we fit into wet pant legs. Mumma keeps an eye on the weather, sometimes dispatching me in a rush to keep an entire load from getting suddenly drenched.

Sister Gemma has dark eyes, prominent dark eyebrows and, from what we can see of it pressed back at her temples by her wimple, dark hair. It's rumored among us kids that she is a convert from Judaism, which exotic origins we think might explain her deep intelligence. Tall — at least to us ten- and eleven-year-olds — and slender, she moves quickly, keeps good order, and teaches every subject in as much depth as we can stand. She mixes up the daily routine with spelling bees and math races. In sixth grade I become the multiplication champ and assume that title into my image of myself.

From Sister we learn that we are never alone because God is always with each of us, no matter what, and knows our thoughts and sees everything — sort of like Uncle George seated at his desk by the window overlooking the Square, a very comfortable idea. When Sister returns from a retreat or conference in Portland, home of the Mercy Sisters' motherhouse, we know to expect some new ideas. Once, she tells us that we must obey our consciences at all times, that if an adult — even one of our parents or one of our teachers — asks us to do anything we know to be wrong we must instead follow our conscience. Another time she tells us that Jesus performed miracles in order to show he was God, not in order to help people. Fifty pairs of eyes look up at her in disbelief. We just know Jesus wanted to help people. Sister doesn't press her case. One day, it must hit her hard that she is up in a backwater rather than down in the big city because, in uncharacteristic exasperation, she pounces on one of us for saying "second of all." "First of all," she tells us, is a proper locution, while "second of all" is not and we get the feeling we've made a sudden drop in her estimation. I'm as caught short as the time in third grade when nice Mrs. Scott during a reading of "The Three

Little Pigs" told our class she never, ever wanted to hear any one of us ever again say "chimley" instead of "chimney."

One day during Religion, Sister states, by the way, that Martin Luther, because he defected from the one true Church, was in hell.

My hand shoots up.

"Yes, Barbara?"

I stand, as we each do when called upon. "Sister, Martin Luther is not in hell. He couldn't be because he followed his conscience."

"He left the Church, Barbara." Sister speaks in a tone meant to convey the last word on the subject.

I remain standing. "But he followed his conscience, Sister. So he couldn't be in hell."

"Barbara," Sister says in a tone that definitely conveys the last word, "Come see me after dismissal."

Ann and others of my friends, accompany me to the after-school meeting eager to see what my punishment will be. I walk to the front of the room where Sister sits behind her desk, her hands interleaved in the sleeves of her habit. Ann and the others remain several steps behind me. Instead of explicating her point of view, Sister asks me to state mine. I give my argument for following one's conscience, a tenet more elegantly stated by St. Thomas Aquinas and taught by Sister herself earlier in the year. Since Sister remains silent, I repeat my position, this time in the flush of intellectual excitement raising my voice and banging my fist on her desk. She lets me go on and on until, I suppose, it's time for her to leave the school building and walk across the yard to the convent.

I will eventually realize that Sister Gemma must have regretted her rash comment about Martin Luther's ultimate end. It wasn't like our elders, however — especially the Sisters — to say they were wrong, although I think maybe it pleased her to see that at least one of her pupils had absorbed her lesson on the primacy of conscience.

I am curious about life in the stately yellow wood-framed building across the yard from St. Mary's School that is the convent. Although I would love to spend a few hours exploring the interior, I don't, as perhaps some of the other girls in my class do, ever entertain the idea of becoming a nun. For one thing, Daddy, although always polite in their presence, does not approve of convent life. "Now a priest," Daddy says, "is his own man. He can drive a car and go about on his own." Nuns, Daddy points out, stick close to the convent, and when they do go out it's two by two. "As though they can't be trusted on their own," Daddy says. "Like children." He says if you meet two of them somewhere — on a train to Portland, for instance — one will do all the talking, the other acting shy as a child. Referring to the nun in charge as "Mother" is another tip-off, Daddy says, that becoming a nun can mean never becoming a grownup. (Some years later when my cousin Mary Alice leaves the Sisters of Mercy after seven years in the order, Daddy will say, "Good, she's done her time!" as though the convent were equal to a prison — or a mental hospital.) Everything about a nun's life from her clothing to her thinking strikes Daddy, who prizes freedom, as restrictive.

Daddy's influence aside, my main reason for not being drawn to convent life is that although the nuns live in community — every one of them assured a passel of "sisters" — I want always to be part of an ordinary, intact family.

Although I never pick potatoes at Cobina's again, Ann and Mary and I love to visit her farm, which isn't too far out of town for us to walk to. Town and county, in fact, are entwined in our thinking and our speech and in the distinctive buildings found in both places. "You couldn't hit the broad side of a barn," we taunt when a snowball misses its mark. "Were you brought up in a barn?" we scold when a friend does something we deem "ignorant." When the whistle blows in the firehouse across the street from St. Mary's School and the engine roars south in the direction of Route One, Cobina offers a silent prayer that her barn hasn't caught fire.

In September in preparation for potato picking, the shacks on Coby's farm fill up with Indians. She takes us to visit Tiny, an old woman she's made friends with. Toothless Tiny, her cheeks as withered and brown as wintered-over apples, tells us stories. As she talks, she pounds an apple against her knee until it's soft enough for her to gum. We look around in admiration at her seasonal home. Colorful throws brighten the sparse furniture. A collie lies next to the wood-burning stove. We envy the freedom the Indians have to move with the seasons, to live off the land, to be at one with nature in a way that we will never be. And yet, we sense a precariousness in their lives that makes us shiver.

Everybody says that Indians won't work more than they have to. They live for the present and that's why, everybody says, they don't get ahead. They love their children and never hit or spank them the way white people do theirs. Unless they've been drinking, that is. Daddy says there are two kinds of people who shouldn't drink — the Indians and the Irish. Everybody says Indian women have unusual endurance. Even women with some Indian blood, like my Aunt Pauline, have unusual endurance.

Coby gets Tiny to teach her some Indian words. When Daddy was a young man and worked shoveling coal with Indians he tried to learn some of their language. "They have no tenses," Daddy says. "Everything's in the present tense. No wonder they can't plan ahead."

Only the Indians speak Indian and only the French speak French — although everyone can say *comment ça va* — but both the Indians and the French speak English. Many of the Indians have French-sounding last names. Quite a few Indians, in fact, are part white — and look white — and quite a few whites have Indian blood. What seems to separate the races isn't theirs looks but their associations and their way of life.

Among whites, there is a communal guilt about Indians that even we children share. Many of the Houlton Indians live on a certain unpaved road where whole families regularly "pick" the nearby dump. Plagued by alcoholism, lack of education and low social standing, they live hand to mouth, never seeming to get

136

ahead, never seeming to live as well as the rest of us. Although there are Indian children at St. Mary's, there are none in Tommy's high school classes, and it will be several years before one finally graduates from Houlton High School.

I get two jobs. One is spending Friday evenings with Nana. She doesn't like to be alone when Grampa goes out to the K of C to play cards. We have a jolly time talking, I stay overnight, and after breakfast with her and Grampa, she gives me fifty cents. My other job is delivering the *Houlton Pioneer Times,* a weekly, on Wednesday afternoons. The McAtees, an old couple at the end of the route, invite me in, offer milk and cookies and usher me to the living room where they have been watching "Pinky Lee." This is before my family has a television of our own, at a time when people of all ages are happy to watch whatever our few channels air.

One Wednesday the paper publishes a salute to its numerous paperboys and "one paper girl." Daddy is delighted by this bit of recognition, but I wish he wouldn't make so much of it because I'm slightly embarrassed to be the only girl in what's clearly a boy's occupation.

Aunt Celia offers to teach Mary Ann and me how to massage backs. Aunt Celia knows about such things because she often goes to doctors, even traveling south to Bangor and Portland to consult with specialists. Daddy laughs with some of the other McGillicuddys, but not Uncle George, at Aunt Celia's various ills and also at the insomnia that causes her to lie abed until as late as nine in the morning and the anxiety that she suffers over picking out Christmas presents or decorating her home. Mary Ann and I go to her house to take lessons. She shows us how to knead and swoop as though we're preparing loaves for the oven. Up to then, my friends and I have scratched each other's backs at pajama parties, and at home we kids sometimes enlist Mumma to scratch our backs. Now I have learned professional massage techniques.

137

Nana McGillicuddy hears of my newfound skills and we decide I might be able to alleviate the pain she feels in her back from sitting most of the day in her kitchen rocker. She leans forward in the rocker and bares her back, careful to shield her breasts — Nana is noted for modesty. On her back is something called a mustard plaster, which I have to peel off before getting to work. Nana almost calls a halt at this point, as though my ministrations would be equal to traveling to Boston and entering a hospital. In the end, she submits to a gentle massage and declares herself much the better for it.

(As for Aunt Celia's putative hypochondria, I realize talking to her years later that she was probably afflicted with endometriosis as well as other gynecological problems and also with a kind of perfectionism that was a byproduct of her artistic nature.)

One day when Mumma and I are home alone, Uncle George walks into the house, greets Mumma cheerily and sits in Daddy's armchair. Unlike his usual dignified self, he's chatty, silly almost. His face is flushed, his expression happy, too happy, happy like a very small child. As he talks, Mumma sits opposite him, a little smile on her face, like the smile she tried to hide when I came home from kindergarten and reported that at the bathroom a boy in my class got his dingy caught in his zipper. Usually, Uncle George makes real conversation, if only about the weather — a subject he knows quite a bit about, actually. But this day he just repeats pointless remarks and says, "What do you say, Mary?" over and over like a little kid. As though she knows she's not part of a real conversation, Mumma doesn't say a whole lot and I only watch. After a while, ten or twenty minutes perhaps, Uncle George stands up with a silly laugh and takes his leave.

Mumma says nothing about this visit, but it's plain to me that, although I've seen Aunt Ruth and Uncle Norman and Cousin George and Lillian drink cocktails, this is my first time witnessing drunkenness in a relative. *Ho, ho, ho, hee, hee, hee, little brown jug how I love thee.* Once, when we lived in Patten, I stood with a crowd of children taunting an inebriated man sprawled on the verge of Mill Pond Road. *Ho, ho, ho....* On Main Street there were men who lay about in a stupor in doorways, the reason being, people said, that they were veterans of the First World War.

Uncle George flew bombing missions in the Second World War. Maybe he feels trapped back home working in his father's business, not exactly his own man. Or maybe he always had a tendency to drink all the way back to his teenaged years when he sought out a more popular, fun-loving set than Daddy did. Maybe he can't get over having to drop out of the University of Maine, to which he feels such allegiance that ever after he stands up and puts his hand over his heart when the Maine Stein Song is played. Maybe he can't get over the baby boy born prematurely, maybe already dead, never drawing even a first breath, his and Aunt Celia's one and only. I don't understand all this the day Uncle George shows up in my house silly drunk; it's what I piece together after I'm grown up. But what I am beginning to understand is that, just as Father Tierney and Sister Gemma say, everyone — not only Daddy — has a cross to carry, and, just as Pollyanna's adult friends demonstrate, everyone at times falls short of our hopes and expectations.

Eventually, Daddy goes to work full time in Uncle Paul's appliance store. At first he works out front. Charming as he can be, Daddy is no salesman. In fact, sharp dealing offends his sense of fair play, and at home he complains of any practices in which he thinks the customer is being taken advantage of. One day he tells us about a family who came into the store to buy a television. Daddy pointed to the young daughter and said, "Instead of buying a TV, you should take your little girl to the dentist and have braces put on her teeth. She's a pretty girl but her teeth stick out like a rabbit's, and as she gets older the other kids in school are going to make fun of her." The family went away without buying a television, Daddy was happy to report. Soon after that, Uncle Paul moved Daddy to the back office where he could put his Houlton Business School education to work.

Daddy is excited about the latest technology, however, and wants our family to have a TV. Uncle Paul even offers to give him one, but Mumma puts her foot down. As the object of charity for the past few years and with outstanding debt we can never hope to repay, we have no business having in our home such a luxury item as a television set. She doesn't spell out these reasons to Daddy — who has no memory of them — just says no in that way she has, leaving him mystified. Not until a few years later when practically every Tom, Dick, and Harry has a TV, does she allow Daddy to bring one home.

Mumma does agree to let Daddy buy tickets for the whole family to attend *Amahl and the Night Visitors,* put on one December by Mr. Rutledge, the town music teacher. "Daddy says this is part of our Christmas celebration," Mumma tells us kids. Two precocious singers, a high school girl and a public school boy my age, play the leads. Mr. Rutledge comes out on stage before the show and explains to us, the audience, how to behave at an opera, such as when it's appropriate to clap. The story takes place in the home of poor crippled Amahl and his mother, who have so little money that his mother attempts to steal from the Three Kings who are spending the night — something Mumma would never do. Caught, the mother isn't punished, and when Amahl offers his crutch as a present for the Christ Child, he is miraculously cured. Although the music slows down the story a little too much for me, it matches my experience to believe that miracles of healing can take place at Christmas.

The following year, when a troupe of wrestlers come to town, Daddy doesn't have to consult Mumma about buying tickets, because she's been hospitalized for a hysterectomy. Also, for some reason, my brothers are not included, and so it costs only two tickets for Daddy and me, neither one of us the sports fans my older brothers are, to see Gorgeous George and company. For years afterwards, Daddy teases me about my reaction to the lady wrestlers, horrifyingly dirty fighters who bit and gouged and sobbed. "I can't look," he says, imitating me, and he throws his hands over his face.

As Daddy settles into a regular job, he stops taking long solitary walks and starts behaving more like other children's fathers. Often at our noon meal on nice summer days, he tells Mumma to pack a picnic supper, and as soon as his work day is finished he drives us out to one of the nearby lakes. While Mumma unpacks our meal onto a picnic table, he swims with us kids. After the swim, we kids grab our towels because, although Daddy doesn't bring one and says towels are for sissies, he isn't above snatching any one he sees lying around and running it over his thick wet hair.

Weekly, Mumma brings home a new armload of library books, fiction and nonfiction for herself, nonfiction for Daddy. Except for Mumma's childhood collection and for our set of *Encyclopedia Americana*, which we consult in fits and starts, we don't own many books. Evenings, our family — minus Tommy who's at the U of M — sit around the living room reading library books. When attacking one, Daddy starts at the beginning, then skips around, going forwards and backwards until he feels finished. (I have told Nana that I peek at the endings of my books, and I continue to do so although she tells me I mustn't.) In winter, the tarpaper Daddy has applied to the house's foundation doesn't keep gusts out, and one or two of us at a time stand over the radiator to get deliciously warm all over. "Scratch my back, please, Mumma," I say if we're standing there together, each reading, and she reaches up under my blouse and runs her nails over my back without taking her eyes off her book. "Stop, Mumma," I say when she absentmindedly starts picking at a mole.

A few Sundays running, Father Tierney urges the congregation to reach into their pockets and pull out "the loose dollar" to add to the collection. This strikes Daddy as very funny. At home, he laughs as he repeats the clever wording — "loose dollar." Same as us kids, Daddy knows to the penny how much is in his wallet and pocket, and Mumma knows what's in her purse. If they borrow small sums from each other, they pay each other back. "Here's the thirty-five cents I owe you," Daddy might say to Mumma, placing a quarter and a dime on the kitchen counter. In our house there are no loose dollars.

When we lived in Woolwich, Daddy found Father Maney's annual report hilarious and once home would reenact it for our benefit. "Have you ever held so much money in your life, Eddie?" he'd mimic the pastor speaking to the rotund, possibly simple-minded, middle-aged man who served Mass as head altar boy. And, yet, despite the healthy bank account, Father Maney regularly urged the congregation to increase their donations. Once, I remember, Mumma and Daddy sat at the kitchen table debating about giving up coffee in order to put more into the collection basket. (Mercifully, considering their already constricted and rapidly dwindling indulgences they didn't do that to themselves.) Father Tierney's appeal does not cause them anguish — possibly because his manner is more pastoral, possibly because they are more realistic about their circumstances, more at peace with themselves.

One evening, a classmate's father pulls into his driveway and remains in the car. After a while, my classmate's mother sends one of the kids out to say supper is ready, and the child discovers that his father is dead, having turned a pistol on himself. About that same time, the father of another classmate dies suddenly. "Dropped dead of a heart attack," people say. "He never knew what hit him." A day or two later, Cobina, Ann, Mary and I, in a mission of mercy, call on Charlene at the dainty little house where her mother has entertained us with such style at birthday and slumber parties. Charlene, admired for her small frame, upturned nose and peppy personality, greets us as happily as ever and chatters away throughout the visit, giving us no opportunity to be sad with her. Afterwards, Coby, Ann, and Mary express surprise at how unchanged Charlene is, as if losing a father is a matter of no consequence. But I know that no matter how unchanged Charlene — and Earl, whose father drowned, and the daughter of the man who committed suicide — may appear to be, losing a father is of great consequence, for I lost mine twice and twice he

142

was returned to me, the time between the loss and the retrieval filled with anguished yearning that for my half-orphaned classmates won't stop until they are reunited with their fathers in heaven. Sister says we shouldn't say we're lucky; God has his plans and luck has nothing to do with it. I know myself to be blessed.

A younger child at St. Mary's, a doctor's son and one of my distant relatives, dies suddenly of undiagnosed diabetes. A paratrooper, home on leave, walks into the Rod and Gun Shop one day, asks to see a gun, loads it and shoots himself in the head. A high school boy stuffs a rag into the tailpipe of his car, sits in the driver's seat with all the windows rolled up and turns on the ignition. A boy Tommy's age enters his parents' bedroom early one morning and shoots his mother dead before she ever wakes up. Indians make a party punch of Koolaid and denatured alcohol and several of them, parents of young children, die. (Daddy says again that although it's okay for a Frenchman to drink, there are two kinds of people who shouldn't.) Regardless of how God conducts our affairs, I'm learning that life is chancy, even though, at present, my family life feels secure.

Over the next few years, Daddy cycles through moods without getting frighteningly high or low. Sometimes when he's feeling good — although he himself says there's such a thing as "feeling too good" — he gets an idea for improving our lot, usually by starting a business or buying a property. He goes to the bank and gets papers he wants Mumma to sign and follows her around the house with them in hand. She doesn't argue with him; she doesn't ever throw up to him the past bad debts and bad judgments that electric shock treatment erased from his mind. Neither does she sign. One day a delegation of men come to the house to talk to Daddy about becoming the manager of their small town a little further north. Daddy is flattered and eager. Mumma won't hear of it.

One proposition that Daddy makes to Mumma every once in a while is that they — we — adopt an Indian child. Maybe he's influenced by Clement's missionary experience in Sister Albert's classroom. Each year the students send money to the African missions and get to supply a baptismal name for a pagan baby. This one year Clement, who enjoys a good income from his paper route, and his classmate Francis, who gets paid for helping out in his father's grocery story, contribute the most, and so the choice of a name for the pagan baby falls to them. They decide on "Clement Francis." Daddy gets a big charge out of this. He posits a scene where in later years Clement goes to Africa and meets the grown up Clement Francis. Every once in a while, out of the blue over the next few years, Daddy will say, "I wonder how Clement Francis is getting along."

Daddy seems to yearn for a local Clement Francis of our own. Mumma tells us kids that Daddy has long sympathized with the Indians' plight. Once, when he was a young man, he said to his parish priest that something should be done — especially for "good Indians."

"Joe," the priest, perhaps a discouraged veteran of Maine Indian Missions, said, "the only good Indian is a dead Indian."

My father tells this story with gusto and with a laugh. Then, imbued with philanthropic ardor, he continues to coax Mumma into adopting an Indian child. With his flair for narrative, Daddy describes the bright, handsome boy who will delight in becoming part of our family and be eternally grateful. Mumma can afford to listen — smile, even — at his entertaining fictions because nothing he says will change her mind. We're not going to adopt an Indian child.

In later years, Mumma will tell me that when Daddy was released from Augusta State Mental Hospital, doctors there told her he must live for the rest of his life in a town where when he walked down the street he saw people he knew to say hello to and that he must keep his ambitions and enthusiasms in check. Always the good patient, the good student, Mumma fully accepts that dictum. For all our sakes, she isn't going to go along with grand plans of Daddy's ever again.

Mumma is so sure of where her responsibilities begin and end that one day after a girl from a neighboring street spends time at our house, Mumma tells me not to invite her back. This other girl is older than I, from a poor home, and has recently lost her mother to cancer. "She's looking for a mother," Mumma tells me, "and I'm not going to be her mother." I'm taken aback that Mumma, who tells us kids to be kind to each other, who regularly reminds me to visit Aunt Kit, who taught me the catechism and my prayers and attends Mass with us every single Sunday, has the freedom of mind to turn aside from this opportunity to practice the virtue of charity.

Daddy, no longer free to pursue his dreams, puts more and more store in his garden, an endeavor that consumes him, a place where— unlike Grampa Vose's plots, which Daddy speaks of scornfully— weeds are never, ever given a chance to take hold. In winter, he consults seed catalogues. By St. Patrick's Day, he starts seeds in pots which he moves around the house to follow the sun. As the days lengthen — Daddy loves the long days, dreads the short winter ones — he turns over the soil in the garden and thinks about how to lay out the plantings. Summer weekdays, he hurries home after his day at a desk to hoe, water, harvest, and replant. Always, to protect his fair skin, he wears long pants and a long-sleeved shirt and a canvas hat with a brim. Unlike Grampa, he doesn't ask us kids to help. The garden is Daddy's project alone. He sinks a defunct, bottomless washing machine into the soft soil and dumps compost into it. He curbs the rhubarb, which has flourished since Davy Watson's time, to make space for raspberry canes. He scythes down encroaching brambles and burdocks, hauls them under the shadow of the bridge and burns them in a leaping bonfire. He becomes an advocate of commercial sprays, greeting each new poison on the market with glee and mourning the ones removed by the FDA. "Black Gold"—he pronounces the brand name while presenting Mumma with a basket of vegetables or a bouquet of flowers. Sundays, after we're home from Mass and have eaten our noontime dinner, he changes from his suit to gardening clothes. As he works, he whistles and sings jolly old songs like "Daisy, Daisy, give me your answer, do" and "You'd look sweet upon the seat of a bicycle built for two," or, plaintively but within the range of normal emotion, the Marian hymn "Mother, Dear, Oh Pray for Me." Once, worried about the state of his immortal soul, I ask Mumma whether it's a sin for him to perform servile labor on Sundays. "For your father," Mumma says, "gardening isn't servile labor; it's recreation."

Now that we have a car of our own — not bought new like the Kaiser-Frazer but second hand —we take Sunday drives. Daddy likes to ride up through Littleton Ridge where he lived as a boy. Then he drives around town so that he and Mumma and we kids can look out the rolled-down windows at other people's gardens and see how they compare with Daddy's. Daddy's is the best garden in town.

Mumma becomes a club woman again. She phones Aunt Pauline, who's too shy to attend meetings of the Houlton Council of Catholic Women by herself, and they go together, Aunt Pauline driving. Eventually Mumma feels well enough off to pay dues to the American Association of University Women. Once more, sandwiches of cream cheese and olives and cream cheese and cherries appear in our kitchen, the ceramic bowl of crusts as tasty as ever. Sometimes she bakes a dessert to take out, and Daddy and we kids feel kind of cheated that it will be leaving our house without our having so much as a taste, but we don't protest too much because we see how happy it makes Mumma to take something nice out to a meeting. Such meetings are never held in our house the way they sometimes were when we lived in Patten, our house — or maybe its inhabitants — not being quite up to club standards.

Daddy joins the Knights of Columbus. Once a year, he and Mumma dress up and attend a ball at the Northland Hotel. When Mumma kisses me good night, she smells of perfume. She's wearing the dangling earrings with little bells on them that Grampa gave her one Christmas in Woolwich. The next morning, she tells me all about the evening — who she and Daddy sat with, what they had to eat, what they talked about. We never keep alcohol at home, but when Mumma and Daddy go to the K of C ball they enjoy one Manhattan apiece because, as Daddy always says, they are not teetotalers. As Mumma talks to me, she's reminded of fancy occasions in Augusta when Daddy was in the legislature. There was a time, before I can remember, when Daddy and Mumma had a busy social life. There may come a day when we kids will, too.

Mumma collects Green Stamps. Daddy despises Green Stamps. When he sees her sitting of an evening at the dining room table licking and pasting them into the booklets the Green Stamp store provides, he deplores aloud how merchants demean housewives. It's a form of chiseling, Daddy says, akin to filing metal off a coin. The customer ends up paying for her own prizes, he says, whereas an honest, straightforward way of conducting business would be to charge less for the products to begin with. When Mumma has enough full books, their pages bulging, their bindings sprung, to buy what she's had her eye on, always something for the house but always of her choice, she walks downtown to the Green Stamp store and returns victorious. Daddy enjoys the new toaster or carving knife or kettle as much as she does. He even turns over to Mumma any Green Stamps a store gives him. But he never stoops to licking, pasting or redeeming.

Charlie and I are playing on our front lawn when Freddie comes along and challenges me to a wrestling match. Soon he and I are rolling on the ground, and just when I think I'm about to pin him, Mumma appears and tells me I must come inside. "You're too old to play like that," she says in the tone of voice that leaves no room for disagreeing. "You're a big girl now."

Nana dies when I'm eleven going on twelve. Weak from heart disease, she spends her last few days at the Madigan Memorial Hospital, run by the Sisters of Mercy. Aunt Carrie, Nana's sister who's a patient there at the same time, dies within days of Nana's passing away, and the family doesn't consider that a coincidence. Congressman Hathaway has appointed Tommy to West Point, and the movie *The Long Gray Line* has come to town. We attend Nana's wake and funeral and the movie all within the same few days. "Ordinarily, we wouldn't be going to a movie at this time," Mumma tells us kids. "We're making an exception because it's about West Point. Nana would understand, but we won't mention it to other people."

I'm in my mid-teens when Grampa Vose dies in the Aroostook Hospital, which we think of as Protestant and which he chose because it had employed the services of the Vose Collection Agency — and so that's all right. Mum goes every day during his short stay and is at his bedside when he passes away.

It will take me until my late twenties to catch up to my feelings about the way my father and grandfather alternately displaced each other, and I will become angry, but when I complain to my brother Tom about Dad's treatment of Grampa, Tom takes Dad's side, explaining that Dad couldn't stand the way Grampa tried to manage him, telling him how to spend his time, what chores to tackle and inquiring into his thinking as though Dad were his child or his employee. "On the other hand," Tom says, "We all feel guilty about Grampa." *We all?* He tells me that once when Grampa was already afflicted with the cancer that would kill him but before he was sick enough to be in the hospital, Tom went to his apartment to borrow his car and found Grampa was in bed and had soiled his sheets. More taken with embarrassment than compassion, Tom accepted the car keys and left without doing anything to help Grampa. I'm shocked by this admission and picture poor, sick Grampa left to clean up after himself unaided. But then I remember that sometime in my own teens I became bored with going on errands with him, bored with traveling around the state with him, bored with Cousin George and my other old relatives. Once, when we were in Waterville, Grampa suggested we drive up Mayflower Hill to Colby and enroll me in the class of 1965. Although fully expecting to go to college — and oblivious to the fact that my potato-picking savings wouldn't begin to cover the cost — I had no idea how the admissions process was conducted, but I was pretty sure it wasn't by showing up with your grandfather and having yourself put on the books. I was mortified at the thought, and Grampa was mystified by my intransigence. In Houlton, although eager to borrow his car for my own purposes, I was no longer his agreeable little companion. Talking with Tom, I realize that as a newly minted adult — and like other adults in my life — I've fallen short of some of my hopes and expectations for myself, and I feel compunction.

I'm on Christmas vacation the morning Grampa McGillicuddy has a heart attack in the shower and dies almost immediately. A freshman at Colby, where, no doubt due to my being a legacy, I've been given a full scholarship, I happen to be looking at Dad that morning when he answers the phone and I see his face go naked. He looks stricken — as we all are, no matter our age, when we know ourselves to be orphaned. I'd packed light, am not prepared to dress for a funeral and that becomes my concern, Grampa not being my father. My father and mother are safely ensconced together in our home — my home still, my anchor and refuge for the years I'm in college, my first two years of teaching, my six-month trek through Europe and my episodic job-and-apartment life in New York City up to when I marry at 28 and begin to think of home as where I live with my husband and eventually our children. And, yet, that earlier home remains as a state of mind. I have retained my Catholic faith, which includes a belief in the Communion of Saints, and so I know myself to be surrounded, like the medieval saint, by a great cloud of witnesses, who provided a place for me to grow up in and who continue to this day to bear me up.

Epilogue

One day in the summer of 2014 I drive around Market Square. The handsome brick buildings are still there — "good bones," someone says of them. New young trees and overflowing flowerpots enhance the sidewalks, but thrift shops have replaced the nice dress shops and elegant drugstores. There isn't much traffic now, motor or pedestrian, and plenty of empty parking places. The town fathers — and mothers — endeavor to keep the spirit of the Square alive. Once a summer The Houlton Water Company sets up picnic tables under awnings and hosts a hot dog feed. Around the Fourth of July, the Chamber of Commerce runs a night called "Midnight Madness" when the remaining stores stay open and vendors fill the sidewalks. At dusk, the swirling crowd halts stock still to watch fireworks from across the river, where a new pedestrian bridge spans the water. On occasion Amish families, newly arrived in The County, set up a farmers' market. A cooperative venture featuring local produce, baked goods, and handmade articles occupies one of the fine old dry goods stores. There's hope that the Square will rise again. In the meantime, commerce has shifted north of town to the odd lots, discount clothing establishments, Walmart's, supersized grocery stores, and twenty-four-hour truck stop that run along Route One off the exit from I-95.

I drive up Main Street past Cary Library to where Main merges with Military. I cross in front of St. Mary's Church, not the New England style white wood building, which burned to the ground on a frigid Saturday night when I was in high school, but the tan brick modern one that replaced it. Straight ahead is Houlton High School, a much-loved alma mater that spawns multiple 5-year reunions summer after summer. I turn down Pleasant Street past Uncle Paul and Aunt Pauline's. Before I get to Nana and Grampa

McGillicuddy's old house I make a right, go through the fairgrounds where an indoor arena has replaced the outdoor rink and to the top of River Street. I follow the street down and down to where a town park and boat ramp have replaced my house and the adjacent snow dump. I drive in and park the car and walk through lush lawn to the water. The Clean Air Act proposed by Senator Muskie and signed into law by President Nixon has revived the waterways of Maine — and of the rest of the country. Each spring, in the spot where Charlie watched two men drown, there's a canoe race, the river fit once again for recreational use. On the opposite bank, a newly groomed river walk extends from the Highland Avenue Bridge a mile or so upstream to the new pedestrian bridge. I walk along my side of the riverbank a short way into the woods where we kids tramped and played and cut down our Christmas trees.

The population of Houlton has shrunk to under six thousand. It's always summer when I'm here now. When our children were young, my husband Frank and I bought a camp on East Grand Lake not far from Uncle Paul and Aunt Pauline's. My children grew up spending the school year in our Brooklyn brownstone, summers at the lake. Now I'm a grandmother and the family I'm thinking about is the one I grew up with.

If I remember correctly, Grampa Vose did the unthinkable by selling some of his AT&T so that Tom could enroll in the engineering school at the University of Maine. The following year, Tom started over at West Point. For the four years he was to be at the Point and the three years immediately after, he and Dina would be unable to get married — more of a disappointment for the two of them than for their mothers. The summer before his plebe year, the summer of Beast Barracks, we six drove to Highland Falls, Dad and Tom alternating at the wheel, Mum exclaiming over the "Falling Rock Zone" signs in New York. On the sultry day after we dropped Tom off, we kids and Dad went swimming in a little lake as warm as spit. I'd been so enchanted by the columns of uniformed marching men that I expressed the wish that West Point would accept women. Dad teased me about that forever after. Back home whenever he asked me to get him a glass of water or wait on him in any other way, he'd jokingly add the military command, "On the double!" Tom wrote long letters home regularly and sent us *Ducrot Peeps,* a jocular account of plebe life and also the catechism of nonsense every plebe had to memorize. "What is a cow?" one of us, out of the blue, would ask the others. Answer: "She walks, she talks, she's full of chalk."

At the end of his first semester, although he made the equivalent of the honor roll, Tom was asked to leave West Point — too many demerits, we kids were told. He switched from the Army to the National Guard and got a job in Connecticut. He and Dina got married that fall at St. Mary's Church in Houlton when he was twenty and Dina, a recent high school graduate, was seventeen. The reception was in the parlor of the Knights of Columbus. "Parents can stand in a young couple's way only so long," Mumma had said. I wore a brown cotton dress with white trim, purchased with potato picking money at Rhines Department Store in Bangor. I loved Dina and was terribly excited. Yet, I had a small, awful realization that my eldest brother and I would never again be members of the same household.

Tom had dismantled his matchbook collection and was surprised when Dina wouldn't allow him to install it in the bedroom of their new apartment. For ten years he pursued simultaneously an engineering degree in night school and an apprenticeship in a tool and die factory. Eventually, he and Dina and their three children moved to the Augusta area, and he became Director of the Small Business Administration for the State of Maine. He had inherited Dad's passion for politics.

Long an avid beer drinker, in his forties he began drinking more heavily and earlier in the day. One day Clem said to me after we'd both been visiting Tom and Dina that he wasn't going to laugh any more at jokes Tom made about drinking. It was as far as either of us was willing to go with this big brother we were still

153

accustomed to looking up to. When, seven years before he was diagnosed with lung cancer, Tom did give up drinking — and smoking — he became characteristically vigorous in his advocacy of sobriety. When he had done all he could to fend off cancer, he embraced the inevitable and hosted a retirement party in the Augusta Civic Center attended by hundreds, including all his first cousins and both Maine Senators, Bill Cohen and George Mitchell. A few months before he died — in a hospice in the Augusta area in 1987 — he rolled onionskin and carbon papers into a typewriter and under the heading "Spuds Special," wrote a final letter to Mum, Clem, Charles and me.

On government loans, Clem attended the University of Maine, where he was a Big Man on Campus. After graduation, he cleared brush for the extension of I-95 into Aroostook County and ultimately got a job writing software in the New York office of the engineering firm that built the highway. He and Linda, a fellow computer maven, married and formed their own company working in the vanguard of the computerization of Wall Street. At forty, they retired from corporate life and, having inherited Dad's fascination with the market, Clem became a private investor. He and Linda live in Florida and the coast of Maine. They have a son and a daughter and two grandchildren. Clem, an avid tennis player, told me several years ago that he's learned to be a graceful loser. "But," he added with a smile, "I still have trouble being a graceful winner."

Charles joined the Army and served two tours in Vietnam as a medic. He says he's about the only person he knows who came out of service in Vietnam — in a field hospital no less — in better mental health than when he went in. He attended the U of M, where he met his wife Ellie. They had four daughters and seven grandchildren. He became an RN and has a master's degree in public health. He is a Civil War re-enactor, a national officer in the Sons of the American Revolution, a member of the VFW and the Grange, and is pursuing membership in the Mayflower Society. Having inherited Dad's passion for social justice, he, with Ellie, sponsored numerous Cambodians immigrating to the United States. Ellie died unexpectedly in the summer of 2012. The following year, Charles retired from Togus, the Veterans Administration Hospital in Augusta, Maine, and the year following that he remarried.

After Mass, during Sunday dinner, Dad often quoted from that day's Bible readings or from the sermon. "In a basket, through a window, down a wall, I was let," he would proclaim gleefully over and over, spellbound by St. Paul's sinuous description of his escape from authorities who would have imprisoned and tortured him. As we kids got older Dad latched onto something from Sirach about being kind to an aged father that seemed meant for our instruction. This business irritated my brothers and me, who saw it as a little self-centered on Dad's part. While Mum encouraged us to leave town in pursuit of education, career, adventure, Dad seemed to be trying to hold onto us. As a young man, he had left his own family to seek his fortune elsewhere. Because of illness, he had taken time off from us as we were growing up. Now, for his own sake, he wanted to hold onto us. It didn't seem fair. But it didn't impede any of us. Although we stayed in close touch with our parents and with each other, we all ventured forth and built lives independent of our family of origin.

Dad's mental problems remained largely in remission from the time he was released from the hospital in Augusta until his children were all adults. Years later Mum said that Dad's doctors told her that most patients as sick as he never left the hospital and that in his case his strong family life made all the difference. When, after Charlie was born, Mum visited Dad at St. Elizabeth's in Washington, D.C., a nurse there told her that when he remembered she was pregnant, a fact he'd forgotten, he began to get better. I've sometimes wondered if the hope that feels innate to my nature would have prevailed if he had not been returned to us and stayed by us. Pollyanna keeps up her glad game until she no longer has the use of her legs, when she despairs until, miraculously, healing begins — which leaves me wondering if the author tacked on this ending in order to stay true to the dictates of stories written for children, despair being too awful a conclusion.

About the time Dad turned sixty, his submerged cyclical ups and downs began to surface once again, politics being a tip-off. Once, expecting a high-minded answer, I asked Mum why he was a Republican when all his brothers and sisters were Democrats. I was shocked when she said it was because he wanted to run for office and Maine was a Republican state. At a time when party loyalties ran deep, he was a loyal member, however, voting the straight party line. Until 1960, that is. He deliberated right up until he stepped into the voting booth and marked the ballot for John F. Kennedy. "Everybody thinks I'm going to vote for him anyway," he said.

By my senior year in high school, Dad's lively but sensible way of talking about politics was veering off course. He fretted aloud about the sorts of global injustices that trouble the souls of saints, artists, and madmen. He conjured grand schemes which he strove to share with people in high office. If I walked into the house and he held up a hand in a shushing motion, his ear held close to the phone with a call in to Senator Margaret Chase Smith, I knew he wasn't exhibiting normal behavior. Mum had said that before he had his first hospitalization, she would look out the window and see him working in the yard with a look on his face that made her frightened for him. Now we kids were frightened for him, too.

After an episode — I don't recall the details — for which he was briefly hospitalized, his doctor prescribed lithium. He remained okay as long as he didn't stop taking this wonder drug. If he happened to miss a dose or two, seduced by the mild mania that ensued he would stealthily stop taking it altogether.

The author Kay Redfield Jamison says that the good feelings associated with mild mania are hard for anyone to give up and the prospect of never achieving that state again difficult to accept. Unfortunately, mild mania, for most people, proves brittle. However long it lasts, it eventually escalates into full-blown insanity, plunging the victim from the heights of mania to the depths of depression, not the blues or the blahs of mild depression but a condition that lands him in bed in the fetal position from which he doesn't rise until suddenly his mood shoots to the opposite extreme. This swinging from pole to pole, this bi-polar wrenching with fewer and fewer temperate respites frightens the sufferer — and everyone around him.

The Christmas I was thirty years old, I stayed on in Houlton for a week or so after my husband returned to New York. Clem was there too. We knew things were bad. Dad was wild-eyed during the day and sunk in on himself at night. One night, he wanted to get into bed with Clem and wrap his arms around him, which was too creepy for Clem, who got up, said he wasn't tired after all and went downstairs. One day, Clem and I stepped out of Woolworth's into a blinding snowstorm and came face to face with Dad. "It's the end of the world," he said as we passed on by each other. County folks might joke that way about the weather, but we could see Dad wasn't kidding. He was spending his days visiting lawyers and other professionals even though he believed that none of them could be trusted, that they were all in cahoots and never had the little fellow's best interests in mind. Funny enough, he was at least partially right. These men were indeed on the phone with each other about Dad along the lines of: *Joe McGillicuddy was just in here — off his rocker again, I'm afraid.* In the window of a travel agency, Dad saw a sign that he came home crowing about. I don't remember the words of the ad but whatever it was, he took them as prophecy and confirmation of the way he'd been thinking all along.

Ever since the day my brother and I walked almost all the way home from Bath and found Dad gone, we'd thought that if we'd

157

been grown up, we'd have known what to do, that Dad's hospitalizations would have been unnecessary if only the family had known how to handle him, how to cure him. Mumma once said, referring to Dad's past illnesses, that some things are too big for a family to handle by itself. I'd never quite believed that. But now Clem and I were adults, we were on the scene, and nothing we did or said was impeding a swift spiral into sheer madness. Dad frightened us.

On Saturday night he got out of bed and roamed the house in his long johns, making crazy talk. He opened the front door, went onto the porch, opened that door and bellowed into the frigid night. I seem to remember that what he yelled was, "Come and get me!" By this time, Clem, Mum and I were all up, sitting in the living room in our bathrobes. When nothing we did calmed Dad, we called the authorities — a doctor, the police, I'm not sure who. Shortly, a doctor and a policeman arrived. They questioned all four of us, Clem, Mum, and me, distraught by this time, and Dad, who had put on his red plaid bathrobe and sat sedately in his armchair, of our whole family group making the sanest appearance.

The doctor gave Dad a shot of a drug we knew he hated because he said it turned a person into a zombie. After it took effect, Dad let himself be led off by the doctor and policeman and was driven to the mental health facility an hour north in Fort Fairfield.

At Mass the next morning, Mum, Clem, and I sat in the front pew as we were accustomed to do so that Mum could hear. It was the Sunday between Christmas and New Year's, the Feast of the Holy Family. The first reading was Dad's oft-quoted passage from Sirach, which hit us as personally as the travel agency ad had struck Dad: "My son, take care of your father when he is old: grieve him not as long as he lives. Even if his mind fail, be considerate with him…"

Over the years, as hearing aids improved, Mum could hear better, although not well enough to manage a classroom. When Title One went into effect in the fall of 1969 and the Houlton superintendent of schools was scrambling to find teachers to fill the new positions, someone in his office thought to suggest Mary McGillicuddy. Sixty years old at the time, Mum went to work at St. Mary's School and stayed for ten years. Tutoring one or two children at a time in math or reading, she was able to bypass her handicap. She was thrilled with the work. "I came alive," I heard her tell a cousin. She was also thrilled with the paychecks. She had worked part-time as curator of our local museum and as a tutor for school children, but this was the first time in over thirty years that she was paid for full-time professional work. Her brother Tom, a superintendent of schools in southern Maine, advised her on paying back into the system and getting credit for her earlier teaching years so that she could qualify for a pension.

About the time Mum went to work as a teacher, a new law went into effect allowing a person to retire at sixty-two and draw Social Security at a lower rate. Dad made up his mind to take advantage. The family warned him against this plan but he was adamant. He had recently had another brush with mental illness and once again a hospital stay in which lithium was reintroduced to set him right. Without the routine of his work week, we feared he'd lose his equilibrium.

Dad's retirement wasn't the disaster we'd feared. He and Mum combined their incomes and divided them equally into his, hers and theirs accounts. With his spare time and spare money, Dad was able not only to follow the stock market but to invest. Having taken charge of the automatic dishwasher some years earlier, he now relieved Mum of laundry duty by driving weekly to the laundromat to use automatic washers and driers. He developed a satisfying daily routine of going to the bank, checking the potato futures, and talking with people around town. He planned little trips to the coast for him and Mum to take on school holidays and vacations. "Look at the two of them," Uncle Clem said to Aunt

Dottie once when he spied my parents arriving for a stay at his seaside rental cottage. "Aren't they just delighted with each other!"

One day Dad went to his doctor to complain about stomach pains. He tried various nostrums before being sent to an oncologist. When the doctor gave a diagnosis, he did not mention cancer by name, and for the first few visits Dad dared not say the word. Finally, he told the doctor that he had cancer insurance. Would this be an appropriate time to activate the policy? Yes, said the doctor.

This happened just about the time Mum retired from teaching. For the next three years Dad was treated in Houlton and also at Mt. Sinai Hospital in New York City. Dad and Mum would stay with Clem and Linda, who were then living in Manhattan. During Dad's hospitalizations, Mum would walk from their Upper East Side apartment to the Met, where she particularly loved the Impressionists, and then on up to spend the rest of the day with Dad, walking back to Clem and Linda's for supper.

Meanwhile, the town of Houlton decided to re-engineer River Street, and our house was condemned. Mum and Dad put their names in for a planned complex of senior citizen housing just the other side of the Highland Avenue Bridge. Mum didn't like leaving her neighbors behind; she felt pushed out, plus she didn't think she was getting a fair price for the house (which she and Dad had purchased from Aunt Celia some years earlier). But she was too busy to give it much thought.

In 1982, at the age of 73, Dad died at Mt Sinai Hospital in New York City. Soon after, I wrote to Mum that I felt as though I'd grown up with two fathers who couldn't get along with each other. She wrote back that the last evening before he died, Dad said to her, "Pa Vose was always good to me. But I wasn't always good to him."

None of us, I've come to realize, was as good to Arthur Garfield Vose as he was to us. When I first came across Carl Rogers's term "unconditional positive regard," Grampa Vose came immediately to mind, and when, my first year out of college,

I was recruited to teach freshmen in a parish Confraternity of Christian Doctrine program and read in Chapter One of the textbook that God was not an old man with a white beard, I was as much taken by surprise as my fourteen-year-old students. Although, once it was brought to my attention, I readily accepted the old-man-with-a-white-beard as an image among images rather than an absolute definition, that particular image, because of Grampa — even though he didn't have a beard — still feels true.

During the last days of Dad's life, time ran out on the house, and the apartment opened up. Uncle Paul and Aunt Pauline and Uncle George and Aunt Celia moved my parents' things — now Mum's things — in, even setting up the cupboards and closets ready for all of us when we arrived for the funeral.

Soon Mum was glad to be in her new place. On River Street she was in the only house on the river side of the street. Except for George and Celia, her neighbors were couples with young children. At "The Highlands" she was part of a neighborly group of older folks, mostly widows. "It reminds me of living in a college dorm," she said. "Except that the first thing we talk about when we meet is what happened to our husbands."

Dad had been the one to follow the stock market, and Mum was surprised to find how well their investments were doing. She said she was sorry she hadn't been willing to listen to all he wanted to tell her about the market. (Once after a grueling operation at Mt. Sinai, the first thing he said on coming to was, "How did the Dow do today?") Left in better financial circumstances than she'd ever before known, she adjusted beautifully. Adding to the stylish garments Linda sent each season, she didn't hesitate to shop on her own. No more waiting for the last markdown on sales, she filled her own clothes closet and also the one in the guest bedroom. After Linda took her to an up-to-date hair stylist in Palm Beach and after agonizing over the decision, Mum switched from her outdated stylist in Houlton, who operated out of her own apartment, to a smart new downtown shop opened by a young couple.

And one more thing. After Mum died, I looked through the basket of what she had called her "important papers" and found a letter with a returned check from the president of a downstate bank. The banker explained that he couldn't accept her money because so much time had elapsed that Dad's debt was no longer on the books. He went on to say something like, "It's people like you, Mrs. McGillicuddy, who make this world a better place." This transaction took place soon after Dad had died; the debt was something he'd have had no memory of.

Mum's apartment complex included a handsome common room, where she took her turn hosting AAUW meetings. She attended events around town and took part in church activities, one being the annual rummage sale where she sorted clothing. "I wouldn't have the least idea how to price things," she said. Having been a stranger in a strange land, she developed the quirk, which Uncle George used to tease her about, of introducing herself after Mass to people from away. After Frank and I bought our camp in 1983, Mum's apartment became the base for town activities for us and our son and two daughters. Winters she traveled south to spend time with her children.

In 1995 at the age of 85, Mum suffered a severe stroke and spent the rest of her life, two and one half years, in a nursing home in Houlton. Rita, a colleague from St. Mary's School, visited her every day. While Mum was still in the hospital Dina drove up from Cape Elizabeth, where she lived with her second husband, to help me close up Mum's apartment. (Possibly the lymphoma Dina was to die of seven years later was even then lying in wait.) After a day of Dina acting as principal charwoman with me assisting, the two of us took a walk, and I told her that after Tom died Mum had changed her will so that Dina would inherit one fourth of her estate. Mum had told me she wanted Dina to have the use of the money for herself and to be the one to decide what to give to her children and when to pass it along. Quietly, Dina said, "Your folks never held West Point against me."

"Why would they?"

"You don't know why Tom had to leave?"

"We were told he got too many demerits." (Although as I grew into adulthood, I did wonder what it was he had done to warrant so many demerits in a short amount of time. I asked him once and knew I was being fobbed off when he laughed and said he'd slept with the Colonel's wife.)

Dina told me the following story: The Christmas of his plebe year she traveled to the Point to spend the holiday with him and was the guest of a military family. At the big dance they were happy to be in each other's arms but frustrated by that being the extent of intimacy allowed them. Hand in hand, they left the dance floor, looking for a spot that would afford them privacy. Down a set of stairs into a basement, they came upon a laundry room. They went in, closed the door and made themselves comfortable amidst a heap of sheets. Passion spent, they fell asleep. When they awoke, it was late, and, worse, the door had locked behind them. They had no choice but to remain where they were until discovered.

Dina said the aftermath was horrible. The family she was staying with didn't speak to her. Her mother had been persuaded to let her go in the first place by their neighbor — and Nana's cousin — Mame Dobbins. Dina felt she'd let everyone down. Tom was told he'd have to leave the Point, although he could return the following fall with the condition that he fraternize with none of his classmates and that until graduation, he would bunk alone and eat in the dining hall at a table by himself. "So that's the story," Dina said. She smiled weakly. "You can tell Clem."

I walk back to the car, get in and sit for a minute looking out. The space doesn't seem large enough for the rambling house and imposing barn that used to be here. Once, when my children were small, a graduate student in psychology spent several sessions at my house in Brooklyn testing some sort of educational hypothesis with my daughters. At the end of her final visit, she said, "You're a wonderfully close-knit family." And then she added, "It won't always be this way, you know. It will have to come to an end."

Once upon a time, everyone I loved most in the world lived in the house at Six River Street. We were a tight-knit family, all together finally after separations and fractures that might never have been overcome. But after only a year or two, our family began to break down again as we kids grew up, went off to college, married and started new families. And even those new bonds have broken down once again — all my parents' grandchildren have grown up and established homes of their own.

I turn the key and drive back out onto the street. A quick left and right and I'm passing the deserted brick building that was once St. Mary's School. I cross the head of Market Square, continue on past the courthouse and out into the country. The farm that was Cobina's doesn't look well-kept anymore. And the barn is gone, long since burnt to the ground. I'm headed back to the lake, south on Route One, which has been straightened and improved so that I'm not going to have to negotiate hairpin turns or suffer the illusion that I'll run smack into a barn.

About the Author

Barbara McGillicuddy Bolton's poetry has appeared in *Echoes Magazine* and *National Catholic Reporter,* her short fiction in *Puckerbrush Review* and *Persimmon Tree.* She contributed a chapter to *Uncovering Teacher Leadership: Essays and Voices from the Field.* In 2015, she self-published a novel, *Lulu Goes to College,* based on her freshman year in college. Barbara grew up in Maine and graduated from Colby College. A retired teacher with three grown children, she and her husband spend summers in Aroostook County and live the rest of the year in Brooklyn, New York.

Barbara McGillicuddy Bolton
mcgillbolt@yahoo.com

CPSIA information can be obtained
at www.ICGtesting.com
Printed in the USA
FSHW020728301119
64384FS

9 781943 424504